PREFACE

1. Scope

This publication provides joint doctrine for planning, employing, and assessing air mobility operations across the range of military operations.

2. Purpose

This publication has been prepared under the direction of the Chairman of the Joint Chiefs of Staff (CJCS). It sets forth joint doctrine to govern the activities and performance of the Armed Forces of the United States in joint operations and provides the doctrinal basis for interagency coordination and for US military involvement in multinational operations. It provides military guidance for the exercise of authority by combatant commanders and other joint force commanders (JFCs) and prescribes joint doctrine for operations, education, and training. It provides military guidance for use by the Armed Forces in preparing their appropriate plans. It is not the intent of this publication to restrict the authority of the JFC from organizing the force and executing the mission in a manner the JFC deems most appropriate to ensure unity of effort in the accomplishment of the overall objective.

3. Application

a. Joint doctrine established in this publication applies to the joint staff, commanders of combatant commands, subunified commands, joint task forces, subordinate components of these commands, the Services, and combat support agencies.

b. The guidance in this publication is authoritative; as such, this doctrine will be followed except when, in the judgment of the commander, exceptional circumstances dictate otherwise. If conflicts arise between the contents of this publication and the contents of Service publications, this publication will take precedence unless the CJCS, normally in coordination with the other members of the Joint Chiefs of Staff, has provided more current and specific guidance. Commanders of forces operating as part of a multinational (alliance or coalition) military command should follow multinational doctrine and procedures ratified by the United States. For doctrine and procedures not ratified by the United States, commanders should evaluate and follow the multinational command's doctrine and procedures, where applicable and consistent with US law, regulations, and doctrine.

For the Chairman of the Joint Chiefs of Staff:

DAVID L. GOLDFEIN, Lt Gen, USAF
Director, Joint Staff

Intentionally Blank

SUMMARY OF CHANGES
REVISION OF JOINT PUBLICATION 3-17
DATED 02 OCTOBER 2009

- Expanded discussion of aeromedical evacuation organization and capabilities including organization of patient movement centers and terminology.

- Updated air refueling capabilities discussion.

- Updated terminology and discussion of air mobility channel missions.

- Revised and updated command and control descriptions, and figures for the global air mobility system.

- Revised director of mobility forces responsibilities and description.

- Revised air mobility planning section, including, Adaptive Planning and Execution system terminology.

- Expanded chemical, biological, radiological, and nuclear discussion as it pertains to air mobility operations.

- Expanded aerial delivery capability discussion.

- Revised operational support airlift guidance.

- Removed reference to air mobility operations control centers which have been phased out.

- Updated terminology throughout publication.

- Updated Glossary Part I "Abbreviations and Acronyms" and Part II "Terms and Definitions."

- Updated References.

Intentionally Blank

TABLE OF CONTENTS

CHAPTER V
AIR REFUELING

CHAPTER VI
AIR MOBILITY SUPPORT

APPENDIX

GLOSSARY

FIGURE

EXECUTIVE SUMMARY
COMMANDER'S OVERVIEW

- **Describes how air mobility operations enable commanders to execute the joint functions of movement and maneuver and sustainment at the strategic, operational, and tactical levels of war.**

- **Explains command and control of air mobility operations.**

- **Discusses planning air mobility operations.**

- **Describes airlift, air refueling, and air mobility support missions.**

- **Outlines the Global Air Mobility Support System.**

General Overview

Air mobility operations are a rapid means to project and sustain power across the globe in support of US national interests and a critical enabler to the US National Military Strategy.

Air mobility is the rapid movement of personnel, materiel, and forces to and from, or within, a theater by air. This includes both airlift and air refueling (AR). The air mobility network combines airlift, AR, aeromedical evacuation (AE), and air mobility support assets, processes, and procedures to support the transport of personnel and materiel.

Rapid global mobility is the timely movement, positioning, and sustainment of military forces and capabilities across the range of military operations.

Deployment

Deployment encompasses all activities from origin or home station through destination, specifically including intracontinental US, intertheater, and intratheater movement legs, staging, and holding areas.

Air Mobility Forces Employment Missions

Air mobility forces conduct employment missions when they airlift units, cargo, or personnel, offload fuel in ground operations, or refuel aircraft during operations. Airlift forces can move combat-loaded units to maximize their readiness for immediate combat operations.

Movement and Maneuver

Air mobility forces enhance other forces' combat power and flexibility, either by extending their range, bolstering their staying power, or providing them with greater maneuverability. Airlift allows deployment of critical early entry force packages over strategic distances without delays caused by terrain or obstacles.

Sustainment

Routine sustainment air mobility missions involve movement of materiel and personnel to reinforce or resupply forces already deployed or employed in operations. Routine sustainment missions also include missions flown in support of military and nonmilitary organizations involved in humanitarian relief operations.

Combat sustainment air mobility operations involve movement of supplies, materiel, and personnel to reinforce or resupply units already engaged in combat. Flight schedules and load plans are usually driven by combat requirements rather than to maximize utilization of allowable cabin loads (ACLs).

Global Mobility Enterprise

The global mobility enterprise (GME) is an integrated series of nodes that support air mobility operations. The four components of the enterprise consist of Airmen, equipment, infrastructure, and command and control (C2). The GME optimizes the capacity and velocity of the air mobility system to support the combatant commanders (CCDRs). The enterprise requires global situational awareness through collaboration, coordinated operations, and adherence to air mobility processes.

Command and Control of Air Mobility Operations

The value of air mobility forces lies in their ability to exploit and enhance the speed, range, flexibility, and versatility inherent in air power.

Centralized control and decentralized execution of air mobility missions are the keys to effective and efficient air mobility operations. Centralized control allows commanders to focus on those priorities that lead to victory, while decentralized execution fosters initiative, situational responsiveness, and tactical flexibility. Although it is not necessary for a single global organization to centrally control all air mobility forces, all commanders should envision air mobility as a global system capable of simultaneously performing intertheater and intratheater missions. Separate but integrated command structures exercise centralized control over United States Transportation Command (USTRANSCOM)-assigned and theater-assigned and attached air mobility forces.

Intertheater, Intratheater, and Joint Task Force Command and Control structures

There are three independent C2 structures that, when integrated, constitute the global air mobility C2 system. They are the intertheater, intratheater, and joint task force (JTF) systems.

Intertheater air mobility serves the continental United States (CONUS) to-theater and theater-to-theater air mobility needs of the geographic combatant commanders (GCCs). Air mobility assets assigned to USTRANSCOM execute the majority of intertheater airlift missions.

Intratheater air mobility operations are defined by geographic boundaries. Air mobility forces assigned or attached to the GCC normally conduct these operations. Intratheater common-user air mobility assets are normally scheduled and controlled by the theater air operations center (AOC) or joint air operations center (JAOC) if established.

JTF Air Mobility Operations. During joint operations, it may be necessary to establish a JTF within a GCC's area of responsibility (AOR). This allows the GCC to maintain a theater-wide focus and at the same time respond to a regional requirement within the theater. When this occurs, a JTF will be designated and forces made available for this operation.

Command and Control of Airfields During Contingency Operations

USTRANSCOM, through Air Mobility Command (AMC), performs single port manager (SPM) functions necessary to support the strategic flow of the deploying forces' equipment and sustainment from the aerial port of embarkation and hand off to the CCDR in the aerial port of debarkation (APOD). The SPM is responsible for providing strategic deployment status information to the CCDR and to manage workload of the APOD based on the CCDR's priorities and guidance.

To facilitate C2 at joint use airfields, the joint force commander (JFC) designates a senior airfield authority (SAA) responsible for safe airfield operations. The SAA controls airfield access and coordinates for airfield security with the base commander or base cluster commander or the joint security coordinator for the area if a base commander has not been designated.

Planning Air Mobility Operations

Joint Airspace Control

Air mobility planners should be involved in the creation of the airspace control plan. Air mobility aircraft typically require preferred altitudes and routing to avoid or mitigate threats.

Air Corridors or Operating Areas

Airlift operations often require secure air corridors or operating areas. These may be shared with other air missions. Regardless, the use of a corridor requires close coordination between the appropriate airspace control authority, the area air defense commander, JAOC, and all other joint force component ground and aviation elements.

Marshalling

Marshalling includes the preparations required to plan, document, and load equipment and personnel aboard the aircraft. The marshalling plan provides the administrative and logistic procedures to accomplish these tasks. The marshalling area is usually located near departure camps and airfields to conserve resources and reduce the opportunity for observation. When the number of departure airfields is limited or when requirements dictate dispersion, loading may be accomplished on a phased schedule.

Intelligence

A joint intelligence preparation of the operational environment effort should be initiated early to identify and assess possible adversary course of action (COA) that could threaten friendly air mobility operations.

The 618 AOC Tanker Airlift Control Center intelligence along with AMC A2 [Directorate of Intelligence] support operational level planning of all USTRANSCOM air mobility missions and coordinates with USTRANSCOM's Intelligence Directorate to fulfill collection and production requirements.

Communications Systems	Communication planning integrates the communications capabilities of joint force components. These plans should include en route communications procedures and automated information systems to support movement reporting; call words or call signs, frequencies, communications equipment, and supplies to be delivered; the sequence of their delivery; and code words for significant events.
Sustainment	Operations and logistics are most effectively integrated as part of a collaborative planning process that includes subordinate component commands, supporting commands, and global providers. Equally important with planning is the active integration of sustainment movements from point of origin to point of need to ensure seamless delivery and retrograde of sustainment cargo. USTRANSCOM develops integrated distribution route structures based on the needs of the CCDRs to ensure timely performance through all segments of the joint distribution pipeline.
Assessment	Assessments must be conducted continuously during air mobility operations. Assessors must ensure that the user's requirement is being met in accordance with established priorities and air mobility forces are being used efficiently and adapting to changes in the operations tempo or focus. Evaluation tools must include metrics to determine on-time delivery amount of cargo/fuel on- or off-loaded and airdrop delivery precision.
	Continuous operational assessment that links operational objectives to airlift tasks is the key to ensuring effective employment of air mobility assets. At the same time, economy of force in air mobility operations has a global impact.
Multinational Planning Considerations	The joint planner should consider complementary multinational capabilities during COA development. However, this capability should be balanced against the potential for competition for US transportation assets to deliver those multinational units into the theater.

Airlift

Airlift is a cornerstone of global force projection.

Within a theater, airlift employment missions can be used to transport forces directly into combat. To maintain a force's level of effectiveness, airlift sustainment missions provide resupply of equipment, personnel, and supplies. Finally, airlift supports the movement of patients to treatment facilities and noncombatants to safe havens. Airlift's characteristics—speed, flexibility, range, and responsiveness—complement other US mobility assets.

Airlift Missions

The basic mission of airlift is passenger and cargo movement. This includes combat employment and sustainment, AE, special operations support, and operational support airlift. The airlift system has the flexibility to surge and meet requirements that exceed routine, peacetime demands for passenger and cargo movement.

Combat airlift missions are missions that rapidly move forces, equipment and supplies from one area to another in response to changing battle conditions. Combat employment missions allow a commander to insert surface forces directly and quickly into battle and to sustain combat operations. Airlift affords commanders a high degree of combat maneuverability permitting them to bypass adversary troop strongholds.

Another important aspect of combat employment and sustainment is the concept of forcible entry. In performing this mission, airlift forces are usually matched with airborne, air assault, light infantry, or special forces specifically designed for delivery by air.

Airland Delivery

Airland is the preferred method of aerial delivery. In the airland delivery method, airlifted personnel and materiel are disembarked, unloaded, or unslung from an aircraft after it has landed or, in the case of vertical takeoff and landing aircraft, after it has entered a hover.

Airdrop

In the various airdrop methods, airlifted personnel and materiel are deployed from aircraft still in flight. Airdrop is often militarily advantageous.

In relation to airland delivery, airdrop delivery has several disadvantages. It carries an increased risk of injury to personnel or damage to cargo. It requires special training for the riggers, transported personnel, and the aircrews. It can limit ACL utilization substantially because of the special rigging required for airdropped materiel. It requires more mission planning time due to the complexity of airdrop operations. If employed by a large formation, it represents an operational level risk.

The JFC makes the decision to continue, cancel, or postpone airdrop operations based on the recommendations of the ground and air component commanders. The airborne force commander and airlift mission commander should coordinate with each other throughout the aerial delivery planning and mission execution.

Air Refueling

AR's contribution to air power is based on the force enabling and force multiplying effects of increased range, payload, and endurance provided to refueled aircraft. AR forces conduct both intertheater and intratheater AR operations.

Air Refueling Operations

Intertheater AR supports the long-range movement of combat and combat support aircraft between theaters, or between theaters and joint operations areas. Intertheater AR operations also support global strike missions and airlift assets in an air bridge. AR enables deploying aircraft to fly nonstop to their destination, reducing closure time.

Intratheater AR supports operations within a GCC's AOR by extending the range, payload, and endurance of combat and combat support assets. Both theater-assigned and USTRANSCOM-assigned AR aircraft can perform these operations.

Anchor Areas and Air Refueling Tracks

AR is normally conducted in one of two ways: in an anchor area or along an AR track. While AR is normally conducted in friendly airspace, missions may require operations over hostile territory and in contested airspace. Anchor areas and tracks may place tankers in an extremely vulnerable position and should be limited to friendly airspace when possible.

In anchor areas, the tanker flies a racetrack pattern within defined airspace while waiting for receiver aircraft to arrive. Once joined with the receiver, the tanker then flies in an expanded racetrack pattern while refueling the receiver. Anchor AR is normally used for intratheater operations where airspace is confined or where receivers operate in a central location.

An AR track is a published track or precoordinated series of navigation points, which can be located anywhere throughout the world. To maximize effectiveness, AR tracks will normally be placed along the receiver's route of flight. AR along an AR track is the preferred method for intertheater operations.

Air Mobility Support

Global Air Mobility Support System

Air mobility support forces provide the responsive, worldwide foundation for airlift and AR operations. This force is divided between USTRANSCOM, which controls the majority of assets in its global/functional role, and the GCCs that control sufficient assets to meet their specific regional needs. These forces, combined with the interrelated processes that move information, cargo, and passengers, make up Global Air Mobility Support System (GAMSS). This structure consists of a number of CONUS and en route locations, as well as deployable forces capable of augmenting the fixed en route locations or establishing operating locations where none exist.

Capabilities of Air Mobility Support

The capabilities provided by GAMSS are C2, aerial port, and aircraft maintenance. While the GAMSS functions at fixed locations are robust, the deployable assets are designed to be temporary in nature with a planned redeployment or replacement.

Command and Control of Global Air Mobility Support System Forces

Air mobility support operations encompass both global/functional support as well as focused regional support. When GAMSS forces deploy to a GCC's AOR, command relationships should be specified, coordinated, and codified before operations begin. They should specify the type and degree of control exercised by commanders in the theater, the providing commander, and the associated C2 organizations.

Global Air Mobility Support System Elements

Several Air Force major commands possess GAMSS elements. AMC GAMSS forces are aligned under the US Air Force Expeditionary Center's administrative control, with assets at fixed overseas locations, as well as CONUS-based deployable assets.

GAMSS fixed assets are sized, manned, and equipped to support peacetime common-user air mobility operation.

GAMSS deployable assets are tailored to meet mission requirements, designed for a decreased transportation and logistics footprint, and are not designed as long-term assets.

Airfield Opening and Global Air Mobility Support System

GAMSS forces may be the first Air Force presence on an expeditionary airfield regardless of how the airfield is gained (e.g., seizure or acceptance from a host nation) or which follow-on US or multinational entity will operate the airfield. When opening an airfield, GAMSS forces normally coordinate actions with theater command elements to ensure theater-specific responsibilities, such as force protection, meet mission requirements.

CONCLUSION

This publication provides joint doctrine for planning, planning, employing, and assessing air mobility operations across the range of military operations.

Intentionally Blank

CHAPTER I
GENERAL OVERVIEW

"...our forces are in distant countries fighting organized terrorists who seek to destroy our nation and destabilize the world. Military operations in these austere places are challenged by the need to deploy and supply troops over great distances. Airlift is a precious lifeline that keeps them fed and equipped, brings the wounded home, and eventually, brings our forces home."

Former Congressman Jim Saxton, 4 April 2005

1. Introduction

Air mobility is the rapid movement of personnel, materiel, and forces to and from, or within, a theater by air. This includes both airlift and air refueling (AR). The air mobility network combines airlift, AR aeromedical evacuation (AE), and air mobility support assets, processes, and procedures to support the transport of personnel and materiel. Air mobility operations are a rapid means to project and sustain power across the globe in support of US national interests and a critical enabler to the US National Military Strategy. The Secretary of Defense (SecDef) directs the assignment of air mobility forces to the Commander, United States Transportation Command (CDRUSTRANSCOM) and other combatant commanders (CCDRs). To deter threats against, or to assist in the defense or pursuit of US national interests, the Department of Defense (DOD) maintains forces, organizations, and processes necessary to conduct air mobility operations. The United States Air Force (USAF) programs the air mobility forces assigned to United States Transportation Command (USTRANSCOM); while USTRANSCOM is responsible for managing the Defense Transportation System (DTS) and overseeing the joint deployment and distribution enterprise (JDDE). Rapid global mobility is the timely movement, positioning, and sustainment of military forces and capabilities across the range of military operations. Air mobility enables commanders to simultaneously execute the joint functions of movement and maneuver and sustainment at the strategic, operational, and tactical levels of war.

2. Deployment

Deployment is the movement of forces into operational areas (OAs) or the relocation of forces and materiel within OAs. Deployment encompasses all activities from origin or home station through destination, specifically including intracontinental US, intertheater, and intratheater movement legs, staging, and holding areas. If these operations must occur in a higher threat environment, tactics, escort requirements, and objective area support requirements could reduce the throughput of the overall air mobility system and limit airlift capacity or AR offload amounts. Commanders and planners should also consider the backhaul capacity of the air mobility forces. Using this capacity for rearward movement of personnel, patients, materiel, and reparable items or the repositioning or redeployment of units can save additional missions from being scheduled or diverted.

Deployment and redeployment are covered in detail in Joint Publication (JP) 3-35, Deployment and Redeployment Operations.

3. Air Mobility Forces Employment Missions

Air mobility forces conduct employment missions when they airlift units, cargo, or personnel, offload fuel in ground operations, or refuel aircraft during operations. Airlift forces can move combat-loaded units to maximize their readiness for immediate combat operations. Given the assumption of immediate combat, user requirements should dictate scheduling and load planning. However, the threat or peculiarities of large-scale operations may dictate adjustments to the user's plans or operations to accommodate the allowable cabin load (ACL) limitations, tactical procedures, and defensive support requirements of the airlift force. AR missions also primarily serve combat air assets directly engaging in combat operations. Fuel loads, flight profiles, and orbits should be determined by combat aircraft requirements. Threats may dictate modifications to the optimum plan in order to protect these limited resources. All air mobility forces can support surge employment operations during the initial stages of a conflict or when required. Commanders should consider the impact that surge operations would have on sustainment and force extraction missions. Backhaul is difficult during this type of mission, as the situation typically limits ground and loiter times and should be limited except for the rearward movement of essential personnel, wounded personnel, or other friendly evacuees.

4. Movement and Maneuver

a. **Rapid global mobility** uniquely contributes to movement and maneuver. Air mobility forces enhance other forces' combat power and flexibility, either by extending their range, bolstering their staying power, or providing them with greater maneuverability. Airlift allows deployment of critical early entry force packages over strategic distances without delays caused by terrain or obstacles. AR extends the range and expedites the arrival of self-deploying aircraft, precluding the need for intermediate staging bases. Airlift and airdrop capabilities allow shifting, regrouping, or movement of joint forces in a theater to attain operational reach and positional advantage.

b. Redeployment air mobility operations involve air movement of personnel, units, and materiel from deployed positions within or between an area of responsibility (AOR) and joint operations area (JOA).

c. Withdrawal operations involve combat air movement of personnel, units, and materiel from positions in the immediate vicinity of adversary forces. The purpose of these movements may range from withdrawal operations to lateral movement of forces to new operating locations. These operations generally are planned to accomplish a movement with the minimum expenditure of air mobility resources. However, in higher threat situations it may also be necessary to preserve the combat capabilities of departing units for as long as possible at the departure terminal, while building them up as rapidly as possible at the arrival terminal. In such cases, operational requirements may be more important than the efficient use of ACLs. In the latter stages of a complete extraction of friendly forces from a combat area, commanders should provide suitable operational assets to protect both the forces being extracted and the air mobility forces engaged in their movement.

5. Sustainment

a. Routine sustainment air mobility missions involve movement of materiel and personnel to reinforce or resupply forces already deployed or employed in operations. Routine sustainment missions also include missions flown in support of military and nonmilitary organizations involved in humanitarian relief operations. These operations normally deliver requirements with the minimum expenditure of air mobility resources. Routine sustainment planning usually assumes user requirements and the general air and ground security situation allow some flexibility in the actual delivery times of specific loads. Flight schedules and load plans are made to maximize throughput from available ACLs and support resources. However, when sustainment channels are operated as part of an integrated, end-to-end distribution process, time-definite delivery (TDD) and interoperable load configurations may drive schedules and load plans. When practical, routine sustainment should be planned to utilize backhaul capacity. Depending on theater and user priorities, typical backhaul loads might include other friendly evacuees, enemy prisoners of war, excess or repairable weapons, and materiel of moderate to high value. In some cases, retrograde movements of repairable items must be planned and executed with the same TDD discipline as sustainment movements to ensure timely return of items to repair facilities.

b. Combat sustainment air mobility operations involve movement of supplies, materiel, and personnel to reinforce or resupply units already engaged in combat. Combat sustainment planning usually assumes requirements and threat situations limit flexibility of delivery times, locations, and configurations of specific loads. Flight schedules and load plans are usually driven by combat requirements rather than to maximize utilization of ACLs.

6. Air Mobility Fundamentals

a. **Airlift Delivery Methods.** There are two basic methods of delivery: airland and airdrop. The delivery method is based on user requirements; type of environment; availability; adequacy; security of airfields, landing zones (LZs), and drop zones (DZs) near the objective area; threats to the objective area; and aircraft/aircrew capability.

(1) **Airland is the most frequently used airlift delivery method.** It permits delivery of larger loads with less risk of cargo loss or damage than the airdrop method. Airland encompasses all situations where personnel and cargo are offloaded while the aircraft is on the ground or, in the case of vertical takeoff and landing aircraft, after it has entered a hover. Although crews normally accomplish offloading from a stationary aircraft with engines shut down, procedures exist to onload or offload with engines running. In situations where the aircrew elects to not shut down engines (e.g., minimum ground time due to high threat, limited ground support), combat offload procedures can be utilized.

(2) **Airdrop** includes all methods of delivering personnel, equipment, and supplies from an airborne aircraft. This enables commanders to project combat power into areas lacking suitable or secure airfields. Airdrops are an alternative when using an

uncontaminated aircraft to deliver mission critical cargo into a chemical, biological, radiological, and nuclear (CBRN) environment; however, the level of airborne contaminants may dictate the aircraft be quarantined and decontaminated upon mission completion. Airdrop enables commanders to capitalize on the element of surprise because of the speed of delivery and the vast number of potential objective areas for the employment of forces. However, the additional weight and space required for parachute rigging and cushioning material reduces the amount of cargo or personnel each aircraft can deliver. The most common means of rigging equipment and supplies for airdrop are the heavy equipment method, container delivery system (CDS), and door bundles. Precision guided rigging equipment should be considered for combat troops operating in austere locations.

The various tactics, techniques, and procedures (TTP) associated with each delivery method are discussed in Chapter IV, "Airlift."

    b. **Aerial Refueling.** AR is an integral part of US airpower. It significantly expands deployment, employment, and redeployment options available by increasing the range, payload, and flexibility of air forces. AR is an essential capability in conducting air operations worldwide and is especially important when overseas basing is limited or not available. Receiver requirements and tanker availability dictate how much fuel can be offloaded, where the refueling will take place, and when the rendezvous (RV) will occur. The receiver aircraft's performance characteristics will dictate AR speed, altitude, and allowable maneuvering during the refueling.

    (1) **AR Anchors and Tracks.** AR is normally conducted in one of two types of airspace: an anchor area or along an AR track. A detailed discussion of tracks and anchors is contained in Chapter V, "Air Refueling."

    (2) **AR Systems.** AR is conducted using one of two systems: boom or drogue. Most USAF and some allied aircraft use boom refueling. United States Navy (USN), United States Marine Corps (USMC), United States Army special operations and refuelable USAF rotary-wing aircraft, and most allied aircraft use drogue refueling. All KC-10s and a small number of KC-135s can also be refueled in-flight. The USN has a limited organic aerial refueling capability using tactical aircraft (e.g., F/A-18 equipped with aerial refueling system) and also utilize contracted AR support (Omega Air). While the USMC has organic KC-130 AR aircraft, these platforms are dedicated and direct support to Marine air-ground task force (MAGTF) operations. Marine KC-130s are not considered strategic or national assets.

    (a) In boom refueling, the tanker aircraft inserts its AR boom into the receiver aircraft's AR receptacle. Boom refueling allows for the rapid transfer of fuel under high pressure to the receiver. This is especially important when passing large quantities of fuel to either large receiver aircraft or multiple fighter-type aircraft.

    (b) In drogue refueling, a hose and basket system is reeled into the air by the tanker aircraft. Receiver aircraft then "plug" the basket with an external probe. Due to hose limitations, fuel transfer during drogue refueling is slower than boom refueling. KC-135 tanker aircraft must have the drogue assembly mounted on the boom prior to flight, and are thus limited to drogue-only refueling while airborne. Therefore, once airborne, most KC-135s can only perform one type of refueling at a time. KC-10 refueling aircraft are equipped with a centerline drogue and an AR boom. They can also be equipped with wingtip AR pods to expand their drogue refueling capability. They can refuel via both methods on the same mission although they cannot do this simultaneously. Additionally, there are a limited number of KC-135 aircraft in the inventory that can be equipped with external wing-mounted pods to conduct drogue AR while still maintaining boom AR capability on the same mission. As noted above, this cannot be accomplished simultaneously. In certain scenarios, this dual refueling capability makes KC-10s and KC-135s with multi-point refueling systems ideal for use as ground alert aircraft. The USAF MC-130 is also capable of providing drogue refueling to rotary wing and tilt rotor aircraft.

c. The AE system provides time-sensitive (TS) en route care of regulated casualties to and between medical treatment facilities (MTF), using organic and/or contracted aircraft with medical aircrew trained explicitly for this mission. AE forces can operate as far forward as aircraft are able to conduct air operations in all operating environments. Specialty medical teams may be assigned to work with the AE aircrew to support patients requiring more intensive en route care.

d. **Scheduling Categories.** For scheduling purposes, air mobility missions are conducted on either a recurrent or surge basis. Recurrent operations establish a scheduled flow of individual aircraft to make the most of available aircraft and Global Air Mobility Support System (GAMSS) assets. Surge operations allow for rapid and substantial movement of cargo and personnel because a large number of assets are committed toward the operation but can only be sustained for a short period of time. Surge operations may

A KC-135R boom type aircraft refueling an F-22.

disrupt the efficiency of the National Air Mobility System (NAMS), require significant regeneration time, and complicate interactions of intertheater and intratheater forces. Geographic combatant commanders (GCCs) request intertheater airlift in support of deployment, sustainment, and redeployment operations through the Adaptive Planning and Execution (APEX) system and Joint Operation Planning and Execution System (JOPES) process. GCCs, in coordination with supporting commanders and Services, establish movement requirements and develop time-phased force and deployment data (TPFDD) in APEX/JOPES. USTRANSCOM, in turn, extracts the movement requirements from the TPFDD, validates the mode of transportation, and forwards the tasking to its components for movement. Intertheater airlift sustainment involves movement of replacement supplies, equipment, and personnel.

Detailed procedures are outlined in JP 3-35, Deployment and Redeployment Operations*.*

   e. **Air Mobility Mission Categories.** The various categories of missions flown are:

      (1) AE missions support the movement of regulated patients with qualified aeromedical air crew members (including civilian specialists with approval), may require special air traffic control (ATC) considerations to comply with patient driven altitude and pressurization restrictions, and utilize medical equipment approved for use on aircraft systems.

      (2) **Channel airlift missions** provide common-user airlift service on a scheduled basis between two or more predesignated points. Channel airlift missions support passenger and cargo movement over established worldwide routes (GCC or Service-validated) that are served by scheduled DOD aircraft under Air Mobility Command (AMC) control or

United States Marine Corps F-18 receiver aircraft using drogue air refueling procedures.

commercial aircraft contracted and scheduled by AMC. The vast majority of airlift sustainment will move on channel missions of which there are two types: distribution and contingency. Distribution channel missions fly on set schedules (e.g., departs every Tuesday at 1200). Contingency channel missions fly on an as needed schedule based on cargo/passenger movement required from/to the predesignated points of the channel. The vast majority of airlift sustainment will move on channel missions. Both types of channel users reimburse Transportation Working Capital Fund (TWCF) based on weight/cube of cargo or a designated cost per passenger. In many cases, channel missions operate as part of an integrated or linked set of movements from point of origin to point of need to consistently deliver requested logistics support when and where the customer requires and meet TDD goals and standards. These TDD goals and standards are key to successful warfighter support. USTRANSCOM, in collaboration with supported CCDRs, establish TDD parameters that may drive channel performance.

JP 4-01, The Defense Transportation System, *provides further details on channel airlift.*

(3) **Special assignment airlift missions (SAAMs)** are airlift missions that are bought by a user to satisfy one or more validated requirements. SAAMs support DOD users as well as other government agencies such as the United States Secret Service, Federal Bureau of Investigation, and Drug Enforcement Administration.

> A "Coronet mission" is a movement of air assets, usually fighter aircraft, in support of contingencies, rotations, and exercises or aircraft movements for logistics purposes. The tanker aircraft in a Coronet mission provides fuel to avoid intermediate stops and provides weather avoidance, oceanic navigation, communication, and command and control of the mission.

(4) **Contingency missions** operate in direct support of an operation order (OPORD). These movement requirements will be identified in a TPFDD listing within APEX/JOPES.

(5) **Chairman of the Joint Chiefs of Staff (CJCS) exercise missions** operate in support of CJCS-directed or sponsored exercises. These movement requirements are also identified in a TPFDD.

(6) **AR missions** provide in-flight refueling to users; for example, foreign military sales, aircraft transfers, and unit moves.

(7) **Training missions** are flown for crew currency and proficiency for airlift AR and AE. A specific type of training mission is the joint airborne and air transportability training (JA/ATT) mission. JA/ATT missions are a joint effort between air mobility units and other DOD agencies to provide for both. These missions may include airdrop, air assault, aircraft load training, AR, and Service school support. JA/ATT missions are part of a Joint Chiefs of Staff (JCS)-directed, AMC-, or theater USAF component command-managed program that provides basic airborne and combat airlift continuation and

proficiency training conducted in support of DOD agencies. These missions include airdrop, air assault, aircraft load training, AR, and Service school support.

(8) **Intratheater common-user airlift missions** provide routine and TS, mission critical support to the GCC and are missions flown by theater airlift aircraft to support common-user theater movement requirements. Intratheater common-user airlift missions are missions flown by theater airlift aircraft to support common-user theater movement requirements.

7. Global Mobility Enterprise

The global mobility enterprise (GME) is an integrated series of nodes that support air mobility operations. The four components of the enterprise consist of Airmen, equipment, infrastructure, and command and control (C2). The GME optimizes the capacity and velocity of the air mobility system to support the CCDRs. The enterprise requires global situational awareness through collaboration, coordinated operations, and adherence to air mobility processes.

a. **NAMS Functions.** The mobility air forces (MAF) are those forces assigned to combatant commands (CCMDs) that provide rapid global mobility and conduct air mobility operations. The MAF's four core functions are airlift, AR, air mobility support, and AE.

(1) Airlift is the movement of personnel and materiel via air mobility forces to support strategic, operational, and tactical objectives. These forces provide common-user airlift between or within theaters. Delivery to destination can be done via airland or airdrop methods.

(2) AR is the in-flight transfer of fuel from an air mobility aircraft to a receiver(s) in support of strategic, operational, and tactical objectives.

(3) Air mobility support is the capability of providing responsive C2 and ground support to air mobility forces worldwide. This capability is provided by a limited number of permanent en route support locations and deployable forces capable of augmenting the fixed en route locations or establishing new en route locations which is known as GAMSS.

(4) AE is the movement of regulated patients between medical facilities by air mobility assets or contracted commercial aircraft. AE patients are airlifted using organic and/or contracted aircraft with medical aircrew trained explicitly for this mission.

AE is further discussed in JP 4-02, Health Services.

b. **NAMS Forces.** NAMS consists of forces that perform intertheater, intratheater, and organic mobility operations. USTRANSCOM and the GCCs possess air mobility assets that are capable of performing both intertheater and intratheater operations. Each Service also possesses some organic air mobility capability.

(1) Air mobility forces under combatant command (command authority) (COCOM) of either CDRUSTRANSCOM or the GCCs provide common-user assets to conduct operations between or within theaters.

(2) The bulk of intertheater air mobility operations are conducted in response to requests from the CCMDs and Services in accordance with (IAW) guidelines set by the President and SecDef. AMC, as the USAF component of USTRANSCOM, is capable of conducting and controlling intertheater air mobility operations across the globe. A unique aspect of these operations is their reliance on GAMSS and the worldwide C2 capabilities of AMC's 618th Air Operations Center (Tanker Airlift Control Center) (618 AOC [TACC]).

(a) The GAMSS is comprised of a limited number of permanent en route support locations plus expeditionary forces that deploy under the global reach laydown strategy. Permanent en route support locations are manned to handle day-to-day peacetime operations. Deployable GAMSS forces can be tailored to augment permanent locations during large-scale contingencies or to establish en route support at new locations where this support does not exist. GAMSS forces enable USTRANSCOM to establish a network of support locations (terminals) linked together by air lines of communications (ALOCs) to create an air bridge. GAMSS forces, by augmenting permanent terminals or establishing new ones, enable airlift aircraft to move personnel, equipment, and supplies to the desired location. Airlift, AR, and GAMSS forces are limited assets; therefore, their use requires detailed and coordinated planning in order to meet validated requirements.

(b) The 618 AOC (TACC) is the C2 node for all USTRANSCOM air mobility missions. Specifically, the 618 AOC (TACC) receives validated common-user requests, tasks the appropriate unit, plans the mission, and provides continuous communications connectivity between intertheater forces, the common-user, and supporting GAMSS forces.

(3) **Intratheater air mobility forces,** normally under the COCOM of designated GCCs or the operational control (OPCON) or tactical control (TACON) of designated subordinate commanders, provide two types of support. General support is provided through a common-user airlift service to conduct operations within the theater or JOA in response to joint force commanders' (JFCs') movement priorities. Direct support may be provided with Service-organic transportation assets in a combat zone IAW the Service component commander's priorities or, one Service component may be tasked to provide direct support to another Service component commander or subordinate commander. Intratheater air mobility operations are conducted in response to taskings from a CCDR or designated subordinate commander and primarily fill theater operational and tactical requirements. Effective and efficient movement and delivery of personnel, materiel, and fuel depend on in-transit visibility (ITV) of assets moving between theaters and extensive coordination between intertheater and intratheater forces. Each GCC has also established a joint deployment and distribution center operations (JDDOC) which is patterned after the USTRANSCOM Deployment and Distribution Operations Center (DDOC). The JDDOC is focused on the GCC's AOR and synchronizes and optimizes the intertheater and intratheater distribution aspects of deployment and multi-modal transfer of resources to integrate the proper mix of flow of forces, materiel, and other forms of sustainment in support of the GCC's missions.

This crucial interaction is fostered by specific C2 arrangements and MAF apportionment both prior to and after a joint task force (JTF) has been established.

See JP 3-30, Command and Control for Joint Air Operations.

(a) Common-user intratheater movements are usually controlled through a theater-specific C2 node, and requirements are met by allocating theater-assigned forces. In United States European Command (USEUCOM), US Central Command, US Southern Command, United States Pacific Command (USPACOM), United States Northern Command (USNORTHCOM), and US Africa Command this node is an air mobility division (AMD) within the AOC. The AMD functions are similar to those of the 618 AOC (TACC). The AMD's theater focus is critical in teaming with the JDDOC or joint movement center (JMC) to coordinate and prioritize the phasing of intertheater and intratheater airlift requirements. The AMD has vast theater expertise and familiarity and is best able to assess theater requirements, allocate forces to meet those requirements, and when needed, seek USTRANSCOM augmentation. Intertheater missions are typically flown to major airfields (terminals) often referred to as "hubs." From these hubs, transported personnel or cargo is distributed by intratheater forces to other terminals, referred to as "spokes" within the JFC's OA.

Chapter IV, "Airlift," provides more details on hub and spoke operations.

(b) Alternatively, when a JTF is established, intratheater movements may be controlled through a JTF-specific C2 node that interfaces with the JDDOC/JMC, AOC's AMD, and 618 AOC (TACC). The JTF-specific C2 node could be a joint, combined, or component AOC as specified by the commander, joint task force (CJTF).

(c) When requirements exceed the capability of assigned or attached forces, JTF air mobility capabilities may be augmented. The supported CCDR may attach additional theater-assigned forces to the CJTF. SecDef may attach USTRANSCOM forces to the supported CCDR, or JFC; USTRANSCOM may support the CCDR by making air mobility capabilities available as a supporting CCDR. Regardless of the source, intratheater, common-user air mobility forces assigned, attached, or made available to a subordinate joint force should be organized under a commander, Air Force forces (COMAFFOR) as appropriate and directed by the theater AOC for optimum efficiency, and effectiveness. The COMAFFOR, joint force air component commander (JFACC) (if designated), and the director of mobility forces (DIRMOBFOR) must ensure intratheater air mobility forces are organized to properly interact with other intratheater and intertheater forces.

(4) **Organic air mobility forces** primarily provide specialized airlift and AR to Service users. Normally, these forces exist as elements of Service or functional component aviation arms and are assigned directly to their primary user organizations. These forces, if assigned to a CCMD, operate under the COCOM of that CCDR. While these forces are not under the control of the USAF component commander, their capabilities and resources should be identified, and operations visible to the 618 AOC (TACC), AMD and, for a GCC, the JDDOC or a JMC which may be established at a subordinate unified or JTF level to support the concept of operations (CONOPS) and COMAFFOR. In special circumstances

under the latter case, these forces may be utilized to augment intratheater forces and accomplish tasks on behalf of their Service or made available for common-user tasking.

c. **NAMS Components.** The NAMS draws its forces and capabilities from both the civil and military air mobility components. Forces and capabilities apportioned to USTRANSCOM, GCCs, and the Services are determined by each organization's requirements for the specialized contributions of each NAMS component. Each component contributes unique capabilities, such as airlifting outsized or oversized cargo or AR other aircraft, or contributes greater efficiencies, such as passenger or small cargo express delivery, that collectively give the NAMS its overall ability to meet the Nation's needs.

(1) The civil component of the NAMS is increasingly called upon to accomplish various air mobility operations. It is therefore prudent for all DOD components of NAMS to maximize their ability to accommodate civil components within the system. The civil component is comprised of civilian airlift carriers who have signed up as members of the Civil Reserve Air Fleet (CRAF). The CRAF is a voluntary contractual program where civil carriers agree to augment military airlift during a crisis in exchange for peacetime defense business. During peacetime, regional contingencies, and major exercises, CRAF carriers voluntarily contract to fulfill personnel and cargo movement requirements. CRAF carriers are contracted daily to fly various categories of airlift, to include channel airlift, SAAMs, exercise support, contingency support, and charter airlift. This augmentation is crucial to all common-users since it allows USTRANSCOM to continue to meet routine scheduled and surge commitments simultaneously. When needed, carriers participating in the CRAF program can be activated in one of three stages with each stage providing greater airlift capacity. These stages include **Stage I**—Committed Expansion (Regional Crisis or Small-Scale Contingency); **Stage II**—Defense Airlift Emergency (Major Theater War); and **Stage III**—National Emergency (Multiple Theater Wars and National Mobilization). **CDRUSTRANSCOM, with SecDef approval, is the activation authority for each stage of the CRAF.** DOD tasks the minimum percentage of assets in each stage necessary to augment military airlift to meet crisis requirements. During activation, USTRANSCOM, in coordination with the civil carriers, exercises mission control over the civil aircraft. CRAF carriers are generally not subject to the same host nation (HN) diplomatic clearance procedures as DOD military aircraft. When necessary and authorized, foreign flag carriers may augment US air carriers.

(2) Commanders and their staffs should be aware that the CRAF may be employed in CBRN high and medium threat areas; however, they will not conduct operations into an airbase that is under attack or contaminated at the time of arrival. Further information regarding joint operations under CBRN threat conditions is available in JP 3-11, *Operations in Chemical, Biological, Radiological, and Nuclear Environments.*

(3) **Additional Contracted Capabilities**

(a) **Tenders.** AMC and Military Surface Deployment and Distribution Command have standardized freight tenders for most modes of transportation. The tender structure allows for companies participating in CRAF the freedom to carry cargo internally or via subcontractors, a practice known as CRAF Prime. Tenders offer many advantages.

These include less than full-planeload movement flexibility, lower overall airlift costs, enhanced economic development (in line with national airlift policy), and swift redeployment. Tender companies also cover beddown and aircrew issues and they enjoy faster overflight clearance processing since they are not usually required to undergo extensive diplomatic clearance procedures. Furthermore, the use of civilian aircraft for military means usually lowers the overall theater presence of the military airlift effort.

(b) **Air Mobility Express (AMX).** At the request of the supported CCDR, the CDRUSTRANSCOM can establish a special channel mission called AMX to move critically needed items rapidly to an AOR. The supported CCDR may apportion part of the CJCS-allocated lift on AMX by pallet positions to each component. For AMX missions to be effective, the supported CCDR should establish a theater distribution system to deliver express cargo from aerial ports of debarkation (APODs) to final destination.

(c) **Theater Express (THX).** Under this construct, GCCs contract commercial air cargo companies to move intratheater cargo in single pallet increments. The THX program is advantageous because it uses civilian aircraft, personnel, and infrastructure to facilitate expeditious movement and engage local businesses. It is cost effective, because each offering is bid competitively between all authorized carriers, and payment is based solely on weight versus contracting an entire aircraft. Therefore, the benefits of THX are multi-fold: the burden on organic airlift and facilitates is reduced, costs are contained and easily and discretely tracked, local businesses are engaged in pursuing US goals, and fewer airmen have to be deployed to build up capacity quickly. Furthermore, contracting by the pallet gives commercial carriers the capability to blend their commercial and military freight, resulting in economies of scale and lower costs.

(4) The military component of NAMS is comprised of active and reserve components of the USAF and organic lift assets in the Army, Navy, and Marine Corps.

(a) **Active USAF component forces conduct routine and contingency air mobility missions in support of all common-user requirements worldwide.** Commanders have full access to these forces, and they are continuously available for immediate worldwide tasking. Most continental United States (CONUS)-based active duty air mobility forces are under COCOM of CDRUSTRANSCOM, and in turn, OPCON of CDRUSTRANSCOM's USAF component, AMC. Similarly, theater-based active duty air mobility forces are under COCOM of their GCC (e.g., Commander, USEUCOM) and, in turn, under OPCON of their respective USAF component (e.g., Commander, United States Air Forces, Europe).

(b) **Air Force Reserve Command (AFRC) and the Air National Guard (ANG) provide vital airlift, AR, AE, and air mobility support capabilities to NAMS.** Their forces possess the same capabilities as active duty forces, and in some cases, unique capabilities not found in the active force (e.g., LC-130). They complement active duty forces during peacetime through a volunteer system. During contingencies or other national emergencies, where requirements exceed the capability gained by volunteerism, these forces may be brought to active duty status either by federalizing guard forces or activating reserve forces. Approximately 50 percent of the air mobility capabilities are resident in AFRC and

ANG. AFRC and ANG personnel are experienced operators and train to the same standards as their active duty counterparts.

Reserve component mobilization is addressed in JP 4-05, Joint Mobilization Planning.

    d. **Air Mobility Operations Considerations**

        (1) **Air mobility is a valuable force multiplier, but to maximize its effectiveness and efficiency users and providers should carefully plan and coordinate its employment.** Its flexibility and vulnerability make it a responsive, but potentially costly, asset to use. The flexibility of the NAMS may, however, be constrained by its logistic support requirements and its dependence on ground equipment for some operations (which may not be available in desired locations or configurations). Properly organized, trained, and equipped air mobility forces can usually be shifted rapidly between missions and terminals. For example, planes and crews dispersed on sustainment missions throughout an AOR can be concentrated for a large formation employment mission. Modern aircraft offer increased mission flexibility because they can be quickly reconfigured for a variety of loads (palletized and unpalletized cargo, rolling stock, passengers, AE, and airdrop loads) or different types of in-flight refueling missions.

        (a) **Operating the air mobility force at its optimal capacity each day should not undermine its timely reaction to unforeseen emergencies or the shifting priorities of an operation or campaign.** Attempts to bank air mobility forces for later missions are usually ill advised because holding them in reserve entails the certain loss of irrecoverable daily transportation productivity.

        (b) **Air mobility aircraft are vulnerable to air and surface attacks.** Similarly, GAMSS units and command elements are organized to provide only for their local security. These vulnerabilities usually mean that optimal air mobility operations are most effective in a low-threat environment. Ideally, friendly air defense forces should protect large-scale or high frequency operations. Air mobility forces can operate in higher threat environments by using aircraft equipped with defensive systems, by using other assets to protect them, or by accepting a possible combination of operational risk, higher loss rates, and reduced efficiency.

Further information regarding local security is available in JP 3-10, Joint Security Operations in Theater.

        (c) When CBRN contamination affects airfield operations, an important contamination control measure available to air mobility planners is use of the exchange zone (EZ) concept. An EZ is a transload base, located beyond the CBRN-threat area, for the transfer of cargo and passengers between uncontaminated (clean) aircraft and previously contaminated (dirty) aircraft. From the EZ, the dirty aircraft shuttle to and from the contaminated APOD to continue TPFDD deliveries. EZ minimizes the number of air mobility aircraft exposed to contaminants and enables continued use of CRAF aircraft when APODs have been contaminated. Further information regarding EZ is found in the *Air*

Mobility Command Counter-Chemical, Biological, Radiological, and Nuclear Concept of Operations.

(d) Split mission-oriented protective posture (MOPP) is a protection measure. Air mobility planners use split MOPP to divide an APOD into clean and dirty sectors, allowing a MOPP reduction in the uncontaminated sectors. If airlift operations must continue into a contaminated airfield, look for clean sections of the runway and/or ramp (upwind of the contaminated sectors) for the conduct of on/offload activities. The contingency response element (CRE) officer in charge at the contaminated airfield should direct the aircrew to clean sectors during ground operations.

(e) CBRN decontamination helps sustain military operations in CBRN contaminated environments by preventing or minimizing mission performance degradation, casualties, or loss of resources. Further information regarding split MOPP and decontamination is available in the *Air Mobility Command Counter-Chemical, Biological, Radiological, and Nuclear Concept of Operations*, and JP 3-11, *Operations in Chemical, Biological, Radiological, and Nuclear Environments*, and JP 3-41, *Chemical, Biological, Radiological, and Nuclear Consequence Management*.

(2) **The Phoenix Raven (PR) program is designed to ensure adequate protection for air mobility aircraft transiting airfields where security is unknown or deemed inadequate to counter local threats.** AMC PR teams will deter, detect, and counter threats to personnel and aircraft by performing close-in aircraft security advising aircrews on force protection measures, accomplishing airfield assessments to document existing security measures and vulnerabilities and assist aircrew members in the performance of their duties when not performing PR duties. PR teams should be considered for all missions that transit high-risk areas. It should be noted that these are limited resources. Therefore, assigning a fly-away security team may be an alternative option if PR teams are unavailable.

(3) **Limited air mobility forces may not be able to fill all demands placed on them.** The scarcity of air mobility assets is a consequence of both their high cost (particularly of aircraft) and of limitations on the dimensions and weight of cargo that individual aircraft or ground support units can handle. Effective and well-coordinated allocation of these assets requires careful prioritization, especially in the face of changing mission requirements. This becomes crucial when distances are long or in the absence of a well-developed surface infrastructure. When time is critical, airlift may be the only choice to ensure the success of high-priority missions. The central problem of theater planning is maximizing air mobility operations for immediate requirements, while also maximizing their contribution to the long-term requirements of the overall operation or campaign. Planners and operators should weigh the immediate needs of the user against the overall requirements and priorities of the JFC. **As a general guideline, airlift forces should not be tasked for movements when surface assets meet shipment requirements.**

(4) **The operational and logistic characteristics of air mobility forces require commanders to:**

(a) Establish priorities for the air mobility effort that reflect national priorities and the CONOPS and intent of the commanders they support.

(b) Monitor and assess air mobility capacity, usually expressed in tons or sorties, on a continual basis.

(c) Specifically task, properly support, and control air mobility forces to achieve desired objectives.

(d) Require air mobility forces to plan their specific missions and transmit required statistical data through the logistics and operational systems.

e. **Force Visibility.** Force visibility shows the current and accurate status of forces at the strategic and operational level; their current mission; future missions; location; mission priority and readiness status. Force visibility provides information on the location, operational tempo, assets, and sustainment requirements of a force as part of an overall capability for a CCDR. Force visibility integrates operations and logistics information, facilitates global force management, and enhances the capability of the entire joint planning and execution community (JPEC) to adapt rapidly to unforeseen events to respond and ensure capability delivery. Force visibility enhances situational awareness and is required to support force sourcing, allocation, assignment of forces; force position; sustainment forecasting and delivery; and forecasting for future force requirements.

(1) **Asset Visibility (AV).** AV is a subcomponent of force visibility. AV provides the capability to determine the identity, location and status of equipment, and supplies by class of supply, nomenclature, and unit. It includes the ability to determine the status of personnel. It provides visibility over equipment maintenance and retrograde actions. It also includes the capability to act upon that information to improve the overall performance of the DOD logistic practices supporting operations. DOD-wide AV requires horizontal integration of supply and transportation activities and one-time data capture. AV includes in-process, in-storage, and ITV. The function of performing AV is a shared responsibility among deploying forces, supporting commands and agencies, USTRANSCOM, and the supported CCDR. Defense Logistics Agency, as Executive Agent for Integrated Data Environment AV and USTRANSCOM with Integrated Data Environment/Global Transportation Network Convergence (IGC), work collaboratively to ensure supply and in-transit data are shared and fused resulting in a complete seamless picture for end-users.

(2) **ITV.** ITV refers to the capability to track the identity, status, and location of DOD units, and non-unit cargo (excluding bulk petroleum, oils, and lubricants [POL]), passengers and personal property from origin to consignee or destination across the range of military operations as part of AV.

For more information on force visibility, AV, and ITV see JP 3-35, Deployment and Redeployment Operations.

f. **Planning Considerations.** Common users directly benefit from understanding the air mobility infrastructure, and becoming familiar with the airlift mission funding categories. Choosing the correct method of delivery, correctly determining whether their requirements can best be served through routine or surge operations, and understanding the funding implications associated with each choice influences the type of support received by the requesting user and also has an impact on the entire NAMS. Therefore users, when submitting their requests, must not only make their choices on an objective analysis of their exact needs, but must also remain flexible as their desires must be balanced against the CJCS priority system and other common-user needs.

(1) **Mission Funding Categories.** Use of air mobility aircraft is funded either through the TWCF or operations and maintenance (O&M) funds. The TWCF program consists of a fee paid by the user to USTRANSCOM via AMC. O&M funding occurs out of the Service component budget with no charge levied directly against the user. The various types of NAMS missions are designed and scheduled according to their funding category.

(a) **Channel Airlift Missions.** Users of channel airlift missions use O&M funds to reimburse the TWCF based on weight/cube of cargo and per passenger from aerial port of embarkation (APOE) to APOD.

(b) **SAAM users** reimburse TWCF at a SAAM rate based on mission flying time, to include positioning (originating station to required APOE) and depositioning (APOD to originating station) legs.

(c) **Contingency Missions.** Users reimburse the TWCF based on mission flying time, to include positioning and depositioning when directly supporting an OPORD, disaster, or emergency.

(d) **JCS Exercise Missions.** Users reimburse TWCF based on mission flying time to include positioning and depositioning.

(e) **AR Missions.** Missions are executed with O&M funds, but the serviced unit pays for the fuel transferred.

(f) **Training missions** flown for currency and proficiency are paid from Service O&M funds.

(g) **JA/ATT missions** are paid by O&M funds that are specifically allocated for joint training.

(h) **Intratheater common-user airlift missions,** flown on USAF airlift aircraft are paid using contingency funding or the TWCF.

(i) **Service Organic Missions.** Missions flown by Service-assigned assets (including other Air Force major commands [MAJCOMs]) to meet their own requirements are paid from Service/MAJCOM O&M funding.

(2) **Air Mobility Infrastructure.** Each type of infrastructure has unique advantages and disadvantages that must be considered when planning air mobility operations.

(a) **ALOCs and Air Terminals.** Establishing ALOCs between air terminals is key to rapid global mobility. ALOCs are air routings connecting a military force with a base of operations that maximize load and fuel efficiencies for airlift, AR, and receiver aircraft while providing a structure to the airflow. An effective ALOCs structure rests on the proper mix of stage and air bridge operations. Stage operations (known to the air mobility community as "lily pad" operations) are typified as missions that originate from a CONUS terminal, delay en route at an intermediate location for refueling, crew stage, and/or crew rest, and terminate at an outside the continental United States (OCONUS) terminal. Air bridge operations are defined as flights between theaters and AORs where the receiver aircraft's range is augmented by in-flight refueling on designated AR tracks. These established routings, air terminals, and AR tracks allow commanders to effectively and efficiently move and position aircraft, cargo, or personnel. Terminals serving ALOCs include ground-based locations where personnel and materiel are either loaded or offloaded. AR tracks are a series of specified points (usually along a receiver's route of flight) where refueling and receiver aircraft conduct in-flight refueling operations. This applies to tankers refueling cargo aircraft, refueling bombers, or assisting in the movement of fighters as part of a deployment.

(b) **Aerial Port.** An aerial port is an airfield that has been designated for the sustained air movement of personnel and materiel as well as an authorized port for entrance into or departure from the country where located. An airfield is an area prepared to accommodate transiting aircraft, (to include any buildings, installations, and equipment). Some air mobility aircraft are capable of operating on unimproved surfaces, but for large operations it is more effective to establish APODs and APOEs on prepared airfields. Prepared airfields are usually preexisting facilities, with hard-surface runways, extensive ground operations areas (for taxiing, parking, cargo handling, and other appropriate uses), and support infrastructure required for sustained operations. These attributes usually make prepared airfields the best available locations for air mobility main bases and the best available terminal for deployment, redeployment, and large-scale employment operations. These attributes limit the number and location of these types of terminals. As a result, commanders should expect these terminals to be targeted by adversary forces.

(c) **LZ.** An LZ is any specified zone used for the landing of aircraft. LZs are usually less sophisticated than airfields, with facilities meeting only the minimum requirements of anticipated operations by specific aircraft. They may vary from isolated dirt strips with no off-runway aircraft-handling areas to hard surface airfields with limited support infrastructure. The main advantage of LZs is that in many cases it is possible to find or construct them near the operating area of supported forces. A close-by, but less sophisticated LZ may offer fewer delays in providing airland resupply to forward-deployed troops or assistance to humanitarian operations. Due to their isolation and possible proximity to threats, operating at these terminals requires significant planning.

(d) **DZ.** A DZ is a specific area upon which airborne troops, equipment, or supplies are airdropped. Although DZs are normally on relatively open, flat terrain, they may be situated on almost any site (including water) suited in size and shape for intact delivery and recovery of airdropped personnel and materiel. The main advantage of a DZ is the ability to deliver forces or materiel when an LZ or airfield cannot be constructed or used because of expense, time constraints, security risks, political sensitivities, or terrain. Similar to LZs, their isolation and possible proximity to threats makes security more difficult. Operations at DZs require significant planning because of limited on-ground support and likely threats to the aircraft and support personnel.

Detailed information on planning air mobility operations can be found in Chapter III, "Planning Air Mobility Operations."

CHAPTER II
COMMAND AND CONTROL OF AIR MOBILITY OPERATIONS

> *"It is no great matter to change tactical plans in a hurry and to send troops off in new directions. But adjusting supply plans to the altered tactical scheme is far more difficult."*
>
> **General Walter Bedell Smith, US Army (1895-1961)**

1. General

The value of air mobility forces lies in their ability to exploit and enhance the speed, range, flexibility, and versatility inherent in air power. Centralized control and decentralized execution of air mobility missions are the keys to effective and efficient air mobility operations. Centralized control allows commanders to focus on those priorities that lead to victory, while decentralized execution fosters initiative, situational responsiveness, and tactical flexibility. Although it is not necessary for a single global organization to centrally control all air mobility forces, all commanders should envision air mobility as a global system capable of simultaneously performing intertheater and intratheater missions. Separate but integrated command structures exercise centralized control over USTRANSCOM-assigned and theater-assigned and attached air mobility forces. This arrangement ensures a smooth interaction of the intertheater and intratheater forces.

a. Effective support of the supported CCDR's mobility requirements demands theater and CONUS-based forces form a mutual partnership. This partnership must operate as an integrated force with interoperable planning, tasking, scheduling, and C2 systems. A critical element of this partnership is linking centralized control agencies such as the CONUS-based forces' USTRANSCOM DDOC and the 618 AOC (TACC) to the theaters' JDDOCs and AOCs. These MAF partners exercise centralized control to ensure the JFC is supported with responsive, capable, and seamless air mobility.

b. **Theater Air Control System (TACS).** TACS is the USAF mechanism for commanding and controlling theater air power for the COMAFFOR. The AOC is the senior C2 element of TACS and includes personnel and equipment of the necessary disciplines to ensure effective control of air operations (e.g., communications, operations, intelligence).

Further details concerning the structure, functions, processes, and personnel within the AOC can be found in Air Force Tactics, Techniques, and Procedures (AFTTP) 3-3, AOC, Operational Employment-Air and Space Operations Center, and Air Force Instruction 13-1AOC series publications.

2. Command Relationships

Effective and efficient employment of air mobility forces requires a clear understanding of the associated command relationships and control processes affecting the application of these forces. Because they may operate simultaneously across three environments: intertheater, intratheater, and within a JTF's JOA, C2 of air mobility forces can be a particularly complex task. Normally, USTRANSCOM forces remain under OPCON of CDRUSTRANSCOM when supporting missions in theater.

3. Command and Control

There are three independent C2 structures that, when integrated, constitute the global air mobility C2 system. They are the **intertheater, intratheater,** and **JTF systems**.

a. **Intertheater Air Mobility Operations.** Intertheater air mobility serves the CONUS-to-theater and theater-to-theater air mobility needs of the GCCs. Air mobility assets assigned to USTRANSCOM execute the majority of intertheater airlift missions. **C2 of these assets is normally exercised by 18th Air Force (AF) through 618 AOC (TACC).** 18 Air Force is the primary worldwide planning and execution agency for activities involving USTRANSCOM-assigned air mobility forces operating to fulfill CDRUSTRANSCOM-directed requirements. Theater-assigned forces also may conduct theater-to-theater air mobility operations. For intertheater air mobility operations, OPCON is normally retained by the CCDR who owns the forces. Specific command relationships for air mobility forces should be established in a manner that best supports the joint tasking and circumstances of the operation.

See JP 1, Doctrine for the Armed Forces of the United States, *for further discussion on command relationships. See the current* Global Force Management Implementation Guidance *for additional information on force assignment, allocation, and apportionment.*

b. **Intratheater Air Mobility Operations.** Intratheater air mobility operations are defined by geographic boundaries. Air mobility forces assigned or attached to the GCC

A typical joint air operations center

normally conduct these operations. Intratheater common-user air mobility assets are normally scheduled and controlled by the theater AOC or joint air operations center (JAOC) if established. The ability to identify and coordinate movement requirements (visible in JDDE-common systems) is critical to providing theater reachback support from the 618 AOC (TACC). When intratheater air mobility requirements exceed the capability of assigned or attached forces, other mobility forces can support intratheater airlift using a support relationship. The supported commander may also request augmentation from SecDef through the request for forces process.

For more information on request for forces/capabilities, see Enclosure R of the Chairman of the Joint Chiefs of Staff Manual (CJCSM) 3122.01A, Joint Operation Planning and Execution System (JOPES) Volume I: (Planning Policies and Procedures).

    c. **JTF Air Mobility Operations.** During joint operations, it may be necessary to establish a JTF within a GCC's AOR. This allows the GCC to maintain a theater-wide focus and at the same time respond to a regional requirement within the theater. When this occurs, a JTF will be designated and forces made available for this operation. The COMAFFOR may be delegated OPCON of USAF assets, and if designated the JFACC, will typically exercise TACON of air mobility forces made available to the JFACC. If the JTF requires additional air mobility forces beyond those already made available for tasking, additional augmentation may be requested.

    (1) The COMAFFOR may appoint a DIRMOBFOR to function as coordinating authority for air mobility with all commands and agencies, both internal and external to the JTF, including the JAOC, the 618 AOC (TACC), and the JDDOC and/or the JMC.

    (2) The DIRMOBFOR

    (a) The DIRMOBFOR functions as coordinating authority for air mobility with all commands and agencies, both internal and external to the JTF. The DIRMOBFOR exercises coordinating authority among theater AOC (or theater JAOC if established), AMCs 618th TACC, and the JMC/JDDOC, for air mobility issues. An essential role for the DIRMOBFOR is serving as the principal interface between the JAOC, the theater's logistics directorate of a joint staff (J-4), and the JMC/JDDOC to ensure appropriate prioritization of air mobility tasks. When a JTF is formed, command relationships for air mobility forces are established IAW the Unified Command Plan and Global Force Management process.

    (b) The DIRMOBFOR will ensure the effective integration of intertheater and intratheater air mobility operations, and facilitate intratheater air mobility operations on behalf of the COMAFFOR. The DIRMOBFOR provides guidance to the AMD on air mobility matters, but such guidance must be responsive to the timing and tempo of operations managed by the JAOC director.

    (c) The DIRMOBFOR also has distinct responsibilities in relation to JFC staffs. Air mobility requirements do not originate in the AOC. They originate at the component level and are validated by either the theater JMC/DDOC (when established) or by the CCDR's operations directorate of a joint staff in coordination with the J-4. This may vary slightly in different theaters. Consequently, an essential role for the DIRMOBFOR is to serve as the principal interface between the AOC, the theater's J-4, and the JMC/JDDOC to obtain appropriate prioritization of air mobility tasks while balancing requirements and air mobility capability.

(3) Specific duties of DIRMOBFOR include the following:

(a) Coordinate integration of intertheater air mobility capability provided by USTRANSCOM.

(b) Coordinate with the AOC director/commander and AMD chief to integrate air mobility operations supporting the JFC into the air assessment, planning, and execution process, and deconflicted with other air operations.

(c) Coordinate with the 18 Air Force/Component Commander (CC) Air Force Transportation Component (AFTRANS) and 618 AOC (TACC) to ensure the joint force air mobility support requirements are met.

(d) Assist in the integration and coordination of the multinational air mobility plan.

4. Command and Control Structures

The air mobility C2 system relies on consistent processes and the ability to rapidly expand to meet the specific needs of the task at hand. This facilitates rapid transition from peacetime to contingency or wartime operations.

a. **Routine Operations.** To assist in the employment of mobility forces, each of the GCCs has a USTRANSCOM transportation liaison officer (LNO). GCCs with assigned air mobility forces have COCOM over those forces and normally delegate OPCON over those forces through Service component commanders. The COMAFFOR executes the C2 of USAF air operations in the theater or AOR through the AOC. One of the AOC divisions, the AMD, usually oversees intratheater air mobility operations. Figure II-1 illustrates these routine, day-to-day command relationships for controlling air mobility forces.

b. **Establishing a JTF.** When a contingency arises, the supported CCDR may elect to establish a JTF and appoint the JFC. The JFC is authorized command authority over a joint force to accomplish an assigned mission and will determine appropriate military objectives and set priorities for the JTF. The JFC establishes appropriate command relationships including those with functional and Service components. The JFC will normally assign JFACC responsibilities to the component commander having the preponderance of air assets and the capability to effectively plan, task, and control joint air operations. If a GCC requires additional air mobility capabilities, the request must be processed through the Joint Staff for SecDef approval.

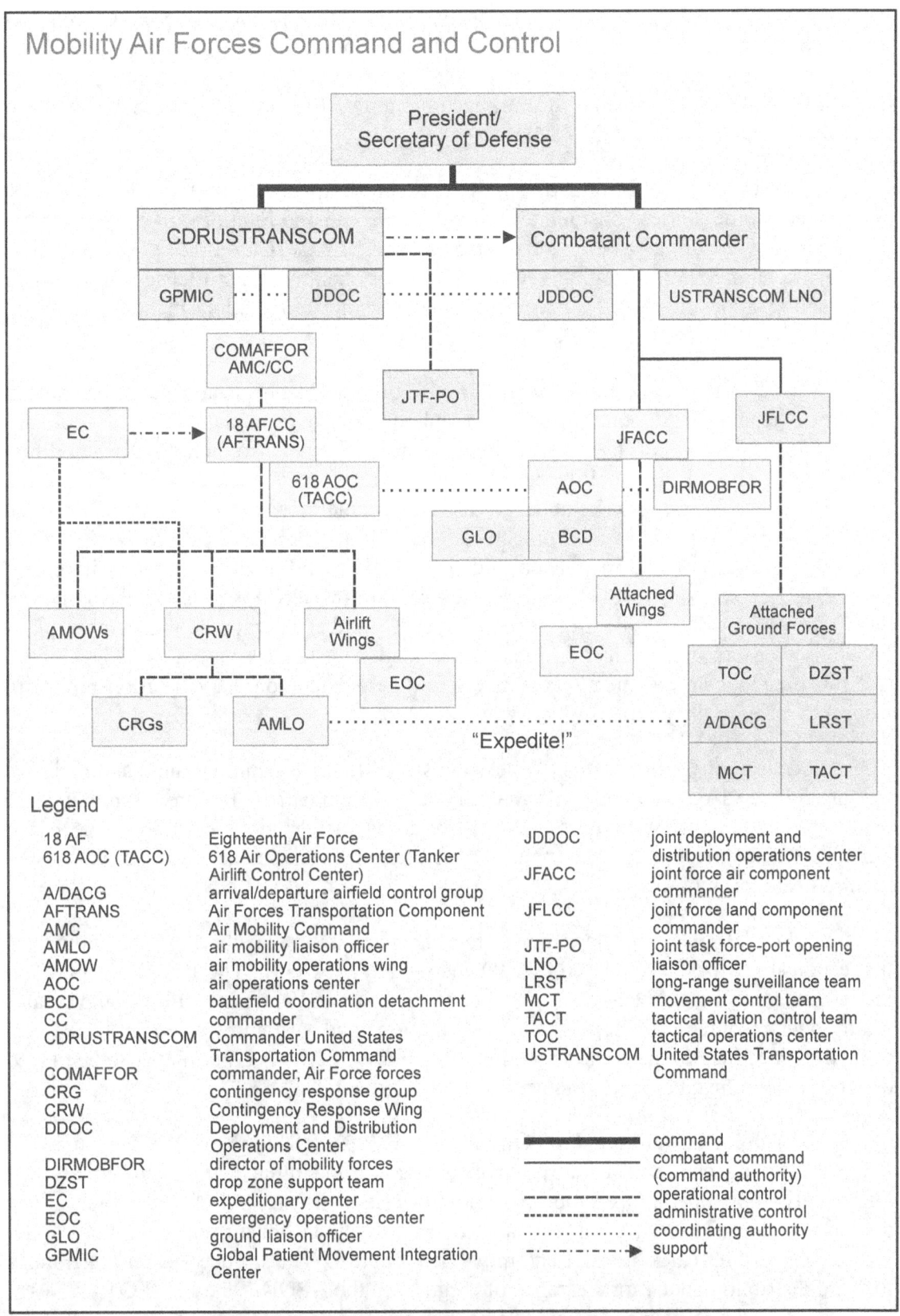

Figure II-1. Mobility Air Forces Command and Control

c. **Establishment of a JAOC and Associated AMC Relationships.** The JFACC requires a C2 organization appropriately sized and tailored to support JTF or subordinate command-related air operations. The JAOC is the air planning and execution focal point for the JTF (or other subordinate command). Centralized planning, direction, and coordination of air mobility operations occur in the AMD.

(1) When a JTF is formed, command relationships for air mobility forces will be established by the JTF establishing authority. The command relationship established for these forces will normally be exercised through the JFACC/COMAFFOR. The JAOC director is charged with the effectiveness of joint air operations and focuses on planning, coordinating, allocating, tasking, executing, and assessing air operations in the OA based on JFACC guidance and DIRMOBFOR coordination.

(2) The AMD is made up of an air mobility control team, an airlift control team, an AR control team, and AE control team, an aerial port control team, a theater direct delivery cell and a mobility support team. Additionally, an AMD may also include a theater direct delivery cell and an air mobility support team. The AMD integrates and directs the execution of theater assigned or attached Service organic mobility forces operating in the AOR or JOA in support of JFC objectives. OPCON of USTRANSCOM-assigned air mobility forces supporting, but not attached to, the JTF or subordinate command will remain with AMC. This expansion of C2 systems requires the AMD to interface with the 618 AOC (TACC), other AMDs if required, and the JAOC combat operations and combat plans divisions to ensure air mobility missions are included in the air tasking order (ATO). Figure II-2 illustrates the arrangement of the JAOC and associated command relationships with respect to air mobility operations.

d. **Additional C2 Structures.** These consist of fixed and mobile units and facilities that provide the JAOC with the information and communications required to monitor the ongoing air operation and control USAF aircraft in theater air operations. The broad organization and functions of these units and facilities are discussed here in their relationship to intratheater air mobility.

(1) **JDDOC.** The integration of intertheater and intratheater movement control is the responsibility of the supported CCMD and USTRANSCOM. The JDDOC is a GCC's movement control organization designed to synchronize and optimize national and theater multimodal resources for deployment, distribution, and sustainment. The JDDOC is normally placed under the control and direction of the CCMD J-4, but may also be placed under other command or staff organizations.

(2) **Joint Task Force–Port Opening (JTF-PO).** USTRANSCOM also provides a JTF-PO to rapidly open and operate ports of debarkation and initial distribution networks for joint distribution operations supporting humanitarian, disaster relief, and contingency operations. The JTF-PO (APOD) consists of an air element for airfield operations and a surface element for cargo transfer and movement control. The surface element operates a forward distribution node for clearance of cargo from the APOD. The JTF-PO (APOD) is designed to arrive early at an airfield to establish single port management and provide ITV from the beginning of an operation. The JTF-PO deploys under the authority of the

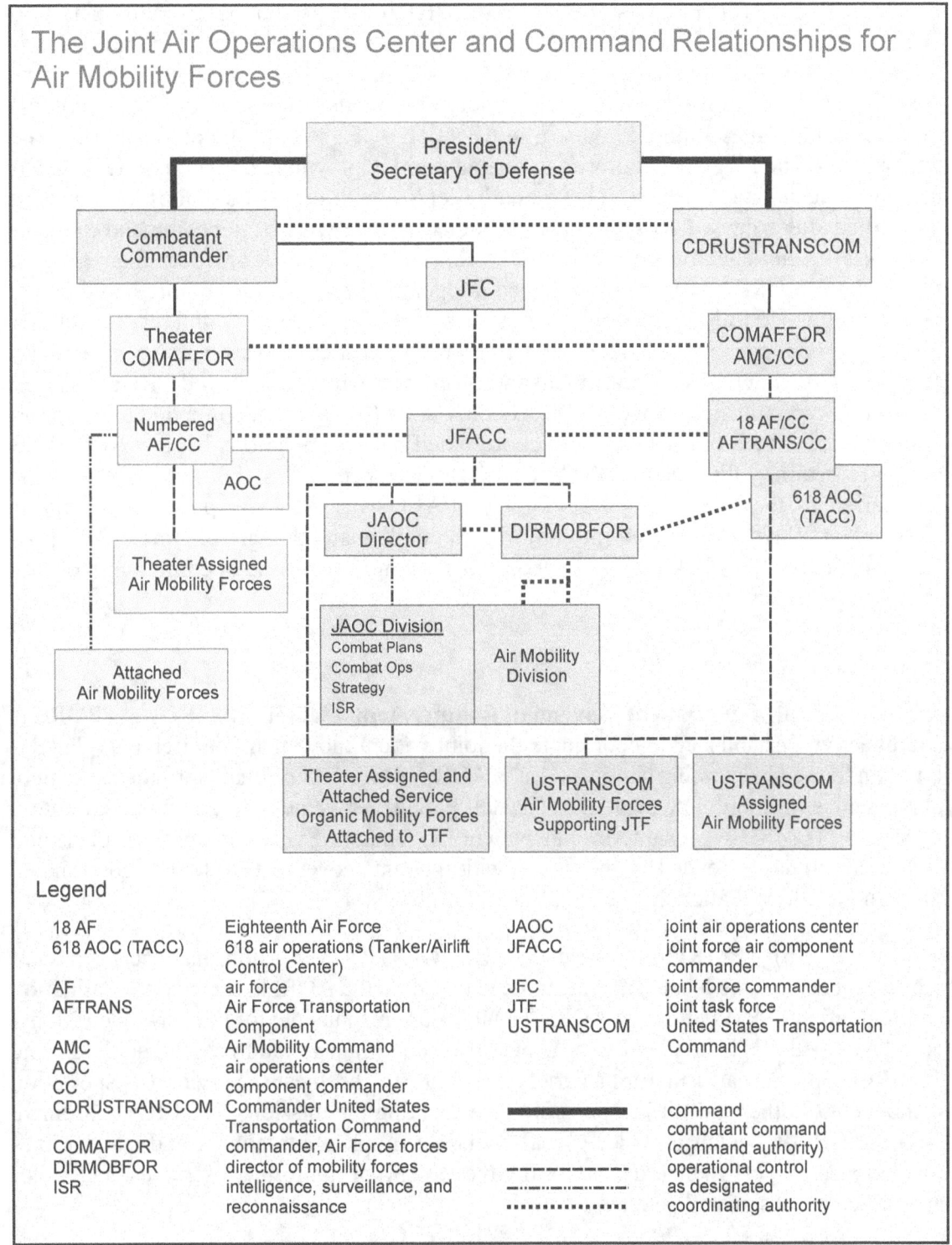

The Joint Air Operations Center and Command Relationships for Air Mobility Forces

Figure II-2. The Joint Air Operations Center and Command Relationships for Air Mobility Forces

CDRUSTRANSCOM, in direct support of the CCDR; it is designed to operate for 45-60 days and be relieved by follow-on forces.

(3) **Contingency Response Forces (CRFs).** CRFs conduct expeditionary port opening operations for USTRANSCOM and GCCs to enable rapid global mobility. CRFs conduct an array of missions including assessing airbase capabilities, opening expeditionary airbases and conducting airfield operations. Active duty CRFs maintain readiness to deploy within 12 hours of notification. CRFs are designed for a decreased transportation and logistics footprint to enable rapid deployment and are not designed as long-term sustainment assets. They usually deploy with organic supplies and must be resupplied after 5 days. CRFs normally coordinate actions with theater command elements to ensure theater-specific responsibilities such as force protection meet their mission requirements. CRFs are normally planned to operate for 45-60 days before handling off responsibilities to follow-on sustainment forces so they can redeploy and reconstitute for subsequent contingency operations. Planners should consider follow-on requirements early on to facilitate timely CRF replacement and coordinate with the deployed CRF to ensure a smooth mission transition. When CRFs deploy to a GCC's AOR, command and support relationships should be specified and coordinated before operations begin. AFTRANS normally retains OPCON of USTRANSCOM-assigned CRFs, but TACON may be transferred to the theater COMAFFOR or JFACC with SecDef approval for unique missions. CRFs are organized into tailored force elements that are comprised of broad cross-section of USAF skill sets to accomplish a range of airbase opening and mobility support operations.

(4) **Patient Movement Centers**

(a) **Joint Patient Movement Requirements Center (JPMRC).** A JPMRC is a joint activity established to coordinate the joint patient movement requirements (PMRs) function for a JTF operating within a GCC's AOR. JPMRCs coordinate intratheater patient movement and coordinate with the Theater Patient Movement Requirements Center–Americas (TPMRC-A) for intertheater patient movement. Synchronization of plans and additional guidance related to the world wide patient movement system is coordinated through the Global Patient Movement Integration Center (GPMIC).

(b) **TPMRC-A.** Located in USNORTHCOM. Additional theater patient movement centers are located and designated based on the AOR, to manage the validation and regulation of PM within the AOR. TPMRCs are responsible for theater-wide PM and coordinate with MTFs to identify the proper treatment/transportation assets required. The TPMRC communicates this transport to bed plan to the theater Service transportation component or other agencies responsible for executing the mission. TPMRCs coordinate with the GPMIC which provides global oversight, implements policy, and standardizes regulations, clinical standards, and safe movement of uniformed services and other authorized, or designated patients.

(c) **GPMIC.** A joint activity reporting directly to the USTRANSCOM Surgeon; serves as DOD's single manager for the development of policy and standardization of procedures and information support systems for global patient movement. The GPMIC implements policy and standardization for the regulation, clinical standards, and safe movement of uniformed services and other authorized or designated patients. The GPMIC orchestrates, and maintains global oversight of the TPMRCs in coordination with the GCCs and external intergovernmental organizations as required. Responsible for the synchronization of current and future operational patient movement plans to identify available assets and validate transport to bed plans.

See JP 4-02, Health Services, *for more information on patient movement requirements center (PMRCs).*

(5) **Emergency Operations Center (EOC).** As the C2 facility of wings, EOCs link wing commanders to the JAOC and enable them to command their forces. To facilitate joint operations, Army ground liaison officers (GLOs) or other component representatives may be assigned to an EOC.

(6) **Control and Reporting Center (CRC).** The CRC is directly subordinate to the JAOC and is charged with broad air defense, surveillance, and control functions. The CRC provides the means to flight-follow, direct, and coordinate the support and defense of air mobility aircraft operating in the OA.

(7) **Tactical Air Control Party (TACP).** TACPs consist of personnel equipped and trained to assist US ground commanders to plan and request tactical air support.

(8) **Special Tactics Team (STT).** STT is compromised of USAF combat control team, pararescue, special operations weather personnel, and selected TACP teams capable of providing terminal control, reconnaissance, and recovery. Special tactics core competencies include austere airfield control; environmental reconnaissance/objective area weather forecasting; terminal attack control/fire support operations; personnel rescue and recovery; battlefield trauma care; and assault zone assessment, establishment and control. In addition, the STT include life support, logistics, weapons, supply, medical logistics, vehicle maintenance, and radio maintenance. These are highly skilled individuals who are technical experts and are worldwide deployable to support any type of contingency. They are uniquely organized, trained, and equipped to facilitate the air-ground interface during joint special operations and sensitive recovery missions. These teams can prepare the operational environment for air mobility operations by conducting survey assessments, weather observations, and reconnaissance and surveillance of objective airfields, DZs, and assault zones. STTs establish terminal area airspace control (attack, C2, and air traffic services) at remote assault (e.g., drop or landing) zones and austere or expeditionary airfields. As special operations forces (SOF), they cannot sustain these operations for long periods of time. Prolonged area terminal airspace control requirements should be handled by the contingency response group (CRG) using organic and augmentee ATC qualified personnel to relieve STTs of this responsibility. When deployed STTs become part of the theater SOF and normally fall under the OPCON of the joint force special operations component commander (JFSOCC) or the joint special operations task force. When supporting theater mobility operations, command authority over STTs should remain in the SOF chain of command. Command relationships and authority should be clearly stated and understood by special operations and air component commanders. STTs are requested from the JFSOCC for tasking.

(9) **The global response laydown team is an air force medical support team that** provides the personnel and equipment required to administer medical care for injuries and illness, and to administer preventive medical care reducing the risk of a catastrophic or detrimental event that could impact on mission effectiveness. The team also recommends strategies to CRF commanders and team chiefs for countermeasures against environmental and physiological stressors, in order to enhance mission effectiveness. While they support deployed CRF operations, the medical support team will be under the same command relationship as the CRF (i.e., if the CRF is OPCON to the JTF, the medical support team should be also).

(10) **Air Mobility Liaison Officers (AMLOs).** AMLOs integrate with supported joint force component staff function(s) at the echelon(s) making decisions for air movement and sustainment planning, validation, prioritization, preparation, and execution. They are organized to advise ground force commanders on air mobility issues and are granted coordinating authority and direct liaison authority to provide essential coordination and enhance the interoperability between the GME, supported CCMDs, joint force partners, and other authorized mobility users in garrison and forward deployed.

(11) **Airborne Elements.** As airborne C2 nodes, the E-2C HAWKEYE and the E-3C Airborne Warning and Control System (AWACS) may perform limited C2 functions in support of theater air mobility operations.

(12) **Army Tactical Operations Centers (TOCs).** TOCs are found in Army units down to maneuver battalions, AMLOs provide input to TOCs at the appropriate echelon depending on the type or phase of an operation, but will normally locate at the division level and above where air movement and sustainment planning, validation, or prioritization decisions are made. Intratheater airlift requests will be validated and prioritized by the Army service component commander.

(13) **Battlefield Coordination Detachment (BCD).** The airlift section of the BCDs will be located within the JAOC and will consist of support personnel organized into airlift, air defense, fire support, and airspace control elements. Overall, the BCD monitors and interprets the land battle situation and provides the necessary interface for the exchange of current intelligence and operational data. The airlift section is collocated with the AMD and is responsible for monitoring movements on joint airlift operations supporting Army forces (ARFOR) and providing feedback to ARFOR operations and logistics staff officers. The airlift section is the single point of contact within the JAOC for coordinating and monitoring Army airlift requests, changes, and cancellations. The other sections coordinate fire and close air support for intratheater airlift missions, as appropriate.

(14) **Army Arrival/Departure Airfield Control Group (A/DACG).** The A/DACG is a provisional organization designed to assist AMC and the deploying unit in receiving, processing and loading or unloading personnel and equipment. A/DACGs are designed to coordinate and control the movement of personnel and materiel through air terminals. The capabilities of the A/DACGs are tailored based on the mission and military units performing aerial port operations. Comprised mainly of personnel and resources from

theater sustainment units along with elements of the moving unit, the A/DACG is task-organized to reflect the type of move and degree of support available at the air terminal. Service transportation support at air terminals assist with the deployment, redeployment and sustainment of forces. Normally, an Army, Navy or Marine Corps A/DACG assists the mobility forces in processing, loading and off-loading deploying and arriving service component personnel and equipment. A/DACGs are deploying Service component's counterpart to an USAF CRG/CRE. When units from more than one component will transit a terminal simultaneously, the JFC should direct one component to provide the A/DACG. This will normally be the component with the largest movement requirement, and augmented, as necessary, by the other components.

(15) **Army Movement Control Teams (MCTs).** MCTs are responsible for coordinating the movement of personnel and materiel from air terminals to their designated destinations. MCTs operate independently of the A/DACG and are responsible for controlling movement on an area basis.

(16) **Army Long-Range Surveillance Teams (LRSTs).** LRSTs can support airlift by conducting reconnaissance and surveillance operations of named areas of interest around terminal areas. LRSTs, which are organized from long-range surveillance detachments and companies, are organic to each Army division. Typically, one to six LRSTs support an airborne or air assault operation. If required, LRSTs can also mark DZs and LZs and direct fire support for airlift operations.

(17) **Army Drop Zone Support Teams (DZSTs).** In the absence of, or in conjunction with, a USAF STT, DZSTs provide Army units with limited organic capabilities to support airdrop operations. DZSTs direct airdrop operations on DZs and consist of at least two personnel, including an airborne jumpmaster- or pathfinder-qualified leader. They can support airdrops (up to three aircraft) of personnel, equipment, and CDS bundles. Their responsibilities include:

(a) Evaluating DZs;

(b) Evaluating ground hazards; and

(c) Ensuring the suitability of the DZ and the ability to recover airdropped personnel and materiel. In the absence of an STT or DZST, AMLOs are qualified to direct airdrop operations.

(18) **Army Tactical Aviation Control Teams (TACTs).** Composed of ATC or pathfinder-qualified personnel, TACTs locate, identify, and establish DZs and LZs. They install and operate navigational aids and communications around the terminal, control air traffic in that vicinity and, to a limited degree, gather and transmit weather information.

(19) **GLOs.** Army units may assign GLOs to the JAOC/AOC and theater airlift EOCs. In those positions, they monitor and report on the current airlift situation to their parent units. They also advise USAF mission commanders and staffs on Army component air movement requirements, priorities, and other matters affecting the airlift situation. GLOs assigned to the JAOC/AOC report through the BCD. They are also the principal points of

contact between the USAF CRGs and A/DACGs for controlling Army theater airlift movements.

5. Command and Control of Airfields During Contingency Operations

a. During contingency operations, efficient and effective use of limited airfield capacity and resources is often critical to a successful military response. The task is complicated when airfields in the theater of operations are host to a variety of allied military, nongovernmental organizations (NGOs), and commercial air activities. USTRANSCOM, through AMC, performs single port manager (SPM) functions necessary to support the strategic flow of the deploying forces' equipment and sustainment from the APOE and hand-off to the CCDR in the APOD. The SPM is responsible for providing strategic deployment status information to the CCDR and to manage workload of the APOD based on the CCDR's priorities and guidance.

b. To facilitate C2 at joint use airfields, the JFC designates a senior airfield authority (SAA) responsible for safe airfield operations. The SAA is trained and certified in SAA duties and responsibilities including ATC and airfield/airspace management and ensures unity of effort among the various commands and other activities operating on the airfield and serves as the arbitrator between competing interests on the airfield. Depending on the types of air operations being conducted at a specific airfield, the SAA will normally be selected from one of the following commands: Army aviation battalion/brigade, USAF expeditionary wings, groups, or squadrons, Marine aircraft wing/group/squadron, USTRANSCOM's CRF, or USAF Special Operations Command special tactics squadrons. The SAA is responsible for overall effectiveness of the airfield and coordination of all requirements for use of the airfield and its facilities. The SAA controls airfield access and coordinates for airfield security with the base commander or base cluster commander or the joint security coordinator for the area if a base commander has not been designated.

(1) In situations where US forces are not the overarching authority for airfield operations (e.g., the HN maintains airfield control, operational civil airfield), the SAA maintains oversight for all US/multinational airfield operations and is the primary negotiator with the respective airfield officials for any support required.

(2) If dual-hatted as the base commander, the SAA has control and responsibility for security operations and will exercise TACON over all forces performing base defense within the base boundary through the C2 mechanism of the base defense operations center (BDOC) (see JP 3-10, *Joint Security Operations in Theater*). The base commander, through the BDOC, addresses threats with attached forces within the designated base boundary, coordinates with the designated area commander(s) for additional support or forces, and if required, requests joint fires within the base boundary. Within this context, clear lines of authority are required to ensure resources and personnel are protected from ground-based attacks and standoff attacks commensurate with the commander's integrated base defense plan.

CHAPTER III
PLANNING AIR MOBILITY OPERATIONS

> *"In preparing for battle I have always found that plans are useless, but planning is indispensable."*
>
> **Dwight D. Eisenhower (1890-1969)**

1. Air Mobility Planning Considerations

a. Mobility aircraft can accomplish a variety of missions. Airlift planning always starts with the requirements. Successful movements start with well defined requirements from the users and may involve significant upfront coordination with lift providers. In short, airlift planning is based on the requirements and the lift planning process is a joint effort between the user and provider that requires lead time and diligence. Therefore, mission planning must include an intelligent application of sound tactical concepts learned from previous conflicts, operational evaluations, training exercises, tactics development programs, and threat analysis. Prior to specific tasking and detailed mission planning, a preliminary study must be done to develop mission profiles and determine the potential for mission success. Feasibility studies are usually done at the joint command level but may be delegated as low as wing level planners. Planners are responsible for providing commanders with accurate assessments during all phases of planning. Most contingency operations will involve joint forces and should integrate the user in mission planning. In addition, planners should include intelligence, C2, escort, security/defense, engineering, combat air patrol, suppression of enemy air defenses (SEAD), service LNOs, weather, maintenance, AE planner and AE patient movement item medical logistics specialist, cargo handlers and inspectors, and airspace controllers. The degree of integration will influence the outcome of the mission. Sharing critical information, especially operational intelligence, between all players clarifies objectives, develops alternatives, and assesses risk. When aircrew, operator, and planner are geographically separated, secure communication is imperative.

b. **Joint Airspace Control.** Air mobility planners should be involved in the creation of the airspace control plan. Air mobility aircraft typically require preferred altitudes and routing to avoid or mitigate threats. Congested airspace and potential fratricide are also major concerns. In addition, air mobility planning considers international, HN, and military airspace control plans and procedures.

Further information on airspace control at the operational level of war, see JP 3-52, Joint Airspace Control. *Further information on terminal airfield ATC, see Field Manual (FM) 3-52.3, Marine Corps Reference Publication (MCRP) 3-25A, Navy Tactics, Techniques, and Procedures (NTTP) 3-56.3, and AFTTP (Instruction) 3-2.23* Multi-Service Tactics, Techniques, and Procedures for Joint Air Traffic Control.

c. **Air Corridors or Operating Areas.** Airlift operations often require secure air corridors or operating areas (e.g., DZ and assault zone run-in and AR tracks). These may be shared with other air missions. Regardless, the use of a corridor requires close coordination between the appropriate airspace control authority, the area air defense commander, JAOC, and all other joint force component ground and aviation elements. Changing of the corridor system may be required depending on the threat lay down and enemy actions.

2. Marshalling

Marshalling includes the preparations required to plan, document, and load equipment and personnel aboard the aircraft. The marshalling plan provides the administrative and logistic procedures to accomplish these tasks. The marshalling area is usually located near departure camps and airfields to conserve resources and reduce the opportunity for observation. When the number of departure airfields is limited or when requirements dictate dispersion, loading may be accomplished on a phased schedule. The USAF component's portion of the marshalling operation is developed during air movement planning and consists of instructions regulating aircraft movement and the parking plan. These procedures are stipulated in appendix 5 (Mobility and Transportation) to annex D (Logistics) of the OPORD.

a. Preparations

(1) **Planning.** The joint force staff coordinates with administrative and logistic agencies for maximum support during marshalling. This support includes transportation, communications, and personnel support functions (campsite construction, operation, and maintenance; messing; and religious, fitness, recreation, and other morale services) and permits the unit to concentrate on preparation for the movement. Support may also include local security personnel to supplement normal USAF security at the departure airfield.

For details on air base defense, see JP 3-10, Joint Security Operations in Theater.

(2) **Logistics.** The unit logistics officer normally prepares the marshalling plan. The plan is an appendix to the service support annex of the OPORD or an annex to the administrative and logistics order of the airlifted force. It should contain procedures for cover and deception. The marshalling plan includes procedures for moving units from marshalling areas through the alert holding and call forward areas to the ready line. Finally, it includes methods for loading troops and equipment into individual aircraft.

(3) **Selection of Marshalling Areas and Departure Airfields.** The selection of marshalling areas and departure airfields is based on the air movement plan and influenced by several common factors. There is no order of priority among these factors, but any one of them could become the basis for final selection. To avoid concentration of forces, multiple marshalling areas and departure airfields should be selected. Excessive dispersion, however, makes C2 more difficult and may diminish the effectiveness of supporting activities. The factors affecting selection of marshalling areas and departure airfields are illustrated in Figure III-1.

(4) **Unit Preparation.** For security reasons, marshalling should be accomplished quickly. To prepare for marshalling, deploying units are responsible for the following:

Factors Affecting Selection of Marshalling Areas and
Departure Airfields

- Mission to be accomplished
- Airfields (number, location, type)
- Air support available
- Communications
- Initial location of participating units
- Vulnerability to adversary action
- Distance to the objective area
- Logistic support required and available
- Unit integrity
- Adequacy of air defense
- Capacity of each airfield to handle sustained operations
- Security requirements, to include camouflage, concealment, and deception measures
- Health hazards and expected weather
- Surface lines of communications
- Types of airlift aircraft used

Figure III-1. Factors Affecting Selection of Marshalling Areas and Departure Airfields

(a) Establish liaison with the departure airfield control group (DACG).

(b) Obtain equipment and supplies as early as possible.

(c) Issue prepackaged supplies and equipment to the airborne forces to expedite loading operations.

(d) Perform final preparation of vehicles and equipment.

(e) Ensure adequate shoring and dunnage materials are readily available.

(f) Receive parachutes and other airdrop items and prepare airdrop loads in coordination with the responsible airdrop support unit.

(g) Prepare and certify aircraft load plans (appropriate USAF officials verify and approve load plans), personnel, and equipment manifests (and annotate any hazardous materials by class), and submit them through the DACG (or designated CCDR agent if no DACG is present) to the supporting airlift elements. As a minimum, manifest information should be submitted electronically, either via disk or direct system interface, to facilitate movement processing and ITV reporting. En route messing is a deploying unit responsibility.

b. **Responsibilities.** Arrival and departure airfield operations are conducted by USAF units and the deploying component units.

(1) CRF teams are responsible for marshalling the deploying unit and associated equipment for airlift. The organization employed depends on the size of the unit being deployed and the number of aircraft involved.

(2) The A/DACG is the deploying Service component's counterpart to the CRG, CRE, or contingency response team (CRT). This organization is sized to support the unit being deployed.

c. **Execution**

(1) The deploying unit assembles, prepares, and documents its cargo and personnel for air movement. Discrepancies are identified and corrected prior to air movement. Departure airfield operations consist of four separate areas of activity. Each activity takes place in a designated area and involves specific tasks. Figure III-2 shows the four separate areas of activity and outlines the major functions of each area.

(2) **Movement to Aircraft Loading Sites.** The deploying commander assigns priorities for deploying unit cargo, vehicles, and equipment to loading sites based on required loading and scheduled station times published in the air movement plan. The deploying unit's installation MAJCOM provides transportation to move personnel and chalk loads (by chalk number) to aircraft. Whenever possible, movements are made at night for operations security (OPSEC) purposes. Personnel in charge of aircraft chalk loads should receive mission briefings concerning the route to their respective aircraft. Personnel and equipment should arrive at onload airfields IAW prescribed times published in the air movement plan. The GAMSS units

Contingency response group loading a C-17 at Hickam Air Force Base.

Departure Airfield Operations

Marshalling Area	Alert Holding Area	Call Forward Area	Ready Line/ Loading Ramp Area
Deploying unit responsibility.	DACG area of responsibility.	Dual DACG and CRF area of responsibility.	CRF area of responsibility.
Prepare vehicles, equipment, cargo, and personnel into chalk loads for delivery to the DACG alert holding area for air movement.	The DACG ensures the movement of vehicles, equipment, and cargo from the alert holding area to the call forward area in orderly fashion.	Joint inspection and discrepancy corrections are conducted in this area.	Receives control of cha ks from the DACG and conducts additional briefings and inspections as required.
	The reception of aircraft loads and conducting preinspections are accomplished here.	Chalk loads are moved from the call forward area and released into the CRF at the ready line.	Responsibility for all air movement operations.

Unit Area

Unit Area

In-check, Assembly and Inspection

Joint Inspections

Unit Area

Final Briefing

Frustrated Cargo Area

Final Manifest Corrections

Major Functions	Major Functions	Major Functions	Major Functions
• In-checks cargo • Prepares personnel and cargo manifests • Prepares other documentation agreed upon during the joint planning conference • Conducts initial inspection of each cha k • Releases each cha k to the DACG at the alert holding area	• Accepts chalk from deploying unit • Conducts inspection • Establishes traffic flow pattern • Establishes communications with deploying units and other functional areas • Provides backup communications with CRF	• Conducts joint inspection • Conducts final briefing and performs final manifest corrections • Compiles statistical data • Provides area for correction of discrepancies identified during the joint inspection	• Establishes aircraft parking plan • Receives load at ready line, directs to aircraft and, in conjunction with aircraft load master or load team chief, supervises the supported component while loading and restraining cargo aboard aircraft

Legend

CRF   contingency response force   DACG   departure airfield control group

Figure III-2. Departure Airfield Operations

control airlift movement at the departure airfield. Routes to and from loading areas should be clearly marked. Strict control of air and ground traffic is maintained on and across runways and strips.

(3) **Preparation of Platform Loads.** If airdrop is part of the operation, platform loads are prepared during marshalling. When planning the preparation and marshalling of platform loads, the following factors should be anticipated:

  (a) Additional lead-time may be required;

  (b) Skilled rigging supervision is needed;

  (c) Materials handling equipment (MHE) required; and

  (d) Adequate facilities, to include a relatively clean and illuminated rigging area, should be provided if tactically feasible.

(4) **Cross-Loading.** Whether administrative or combat-loaded, aircraft also may be cross-loaded. **Cross-loading distributes supplies and/or personnel among aircraft to ensure the entire supply of one item or unit is not lost by an abort or loss of one or a few aircraft.** Cross-loading does not alter the desirability of keeping ground force crews in the same aircraft as their vehicles, weapon systems, or other crew-served equipment.

(5) **Arrival Airfield Operations.** Although arrival operations are not part of the marshalling process, they are important in air movement. If not orderly, arrival operations could adversely affect the mission. Arrival operations take place in three main areas: the offloading ramp, the holding area, and unit area and begins the "reception" segment of the joint reception, staging, onward movement, and integration (JRSOI) phase of deployment operations. JRSOI is the essential process that transitions deploying forces, consisting of personnel, equipment, and materiel arriving in theater, into forces capable of meeting the CCDR's operational requirements. Reception operations include all those functions required to receive and clear personnel, equipment, and materiel through the port of debarkation. This process may be modified or streamlined for combat offload operations. Figure III-3 shows a typical layout of arrival airfield operations.

For more information on the JRSOI phase of the deployment process, see JP 3-35, Deployment and Redeployment Operations.

(6) **Unit commanders or team chiefs coordinate** with the A/DACG for use of available facilities and areas at departure airfields for a command post, communications centers, briefing areas, and equipment and supply handling points.

3. Intelligence

Intelligence is fundamental to effective planning, security, and deception. The intelligence planning effort must be focused to ensure it is responsive to the commander's requirements and the requirements of the subordinate units. To ensure the intelligence effort addresses the commander's needs and is fully synchronized with operations, it is imperative the appropriate intelligence staff elements be fully involved in the operations planning process from the outset. Pertinent information must be analyzed concerning the operational environment pertaining to potential threats. Information shortfalls and the commander's critical information requirements must be identified early, converted into intelligence

Arrival Airfield Operations

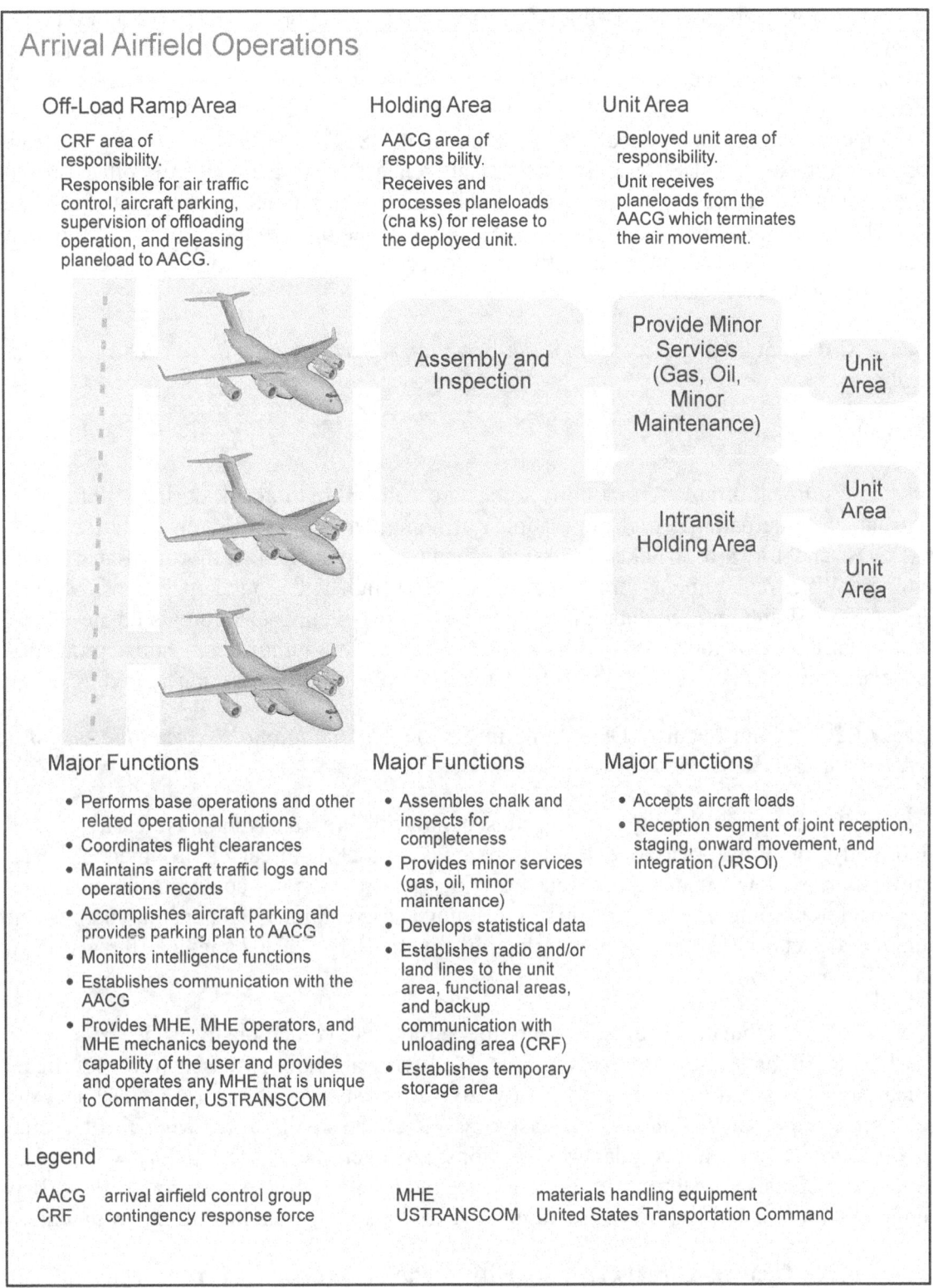

Off-Load Ramp Area

CRF area of responsibility.

Responsible for air traffic control, aircraft parking, supervision of offloading operation, and releasing planeload to AACG.

Holding Area

AACG area of respons bility.

Receives and processes planeloads (cha ks) for release to the deployed unit.

Unit Area

Deployed unit area of responsibility.

Unit receives planeloads from the AACG which terminates the air movement.

Assembly and Inspection

Provide Minor Services (Gas, Oil, Minor Maintenance)

Unit Area

Intransit Holding Area

Unit Area

Unit Area

Major Functions

- Performs base operations and other related operational functions
- Coordinates flight clearances
- Maintains aircraft traffic logs and operations records
- Accomplishes aircraft parking and provides parking plan to AACG
- Monitors intelligence functions
- Establishes communication with the AACG
- Provides MHE, MHE operators, and MHE mechanics beyond the capability of the user and provides and operates any MHE that is unique to Commander, USTRANSCOM

Major Functions

- Assembles chalk and inspects for completeness
- Provides minor services (gas, oil, minor maintenance)
- Develops statistical data
- Establishes radio and/or land lines to the unit area, functional areas, and backup communication with unloading area (CRF)
- Establishes temporary storage area

Major Functions

- Accepts aircraft loads
- Reception segment of joint reception, staging, onward movement, and integration (JRSOI)

Legend

AACG	arrival airfield control group	MHE	materials handling equipment
CRF	contingency response force	USTRANSCOM	United States Transportation Command

Figure III-3. Arrival Airfield Operations

requirements, and submitted for collection or production as requests for information. A joint intelligence preparation of the operational environment (JIPOE) effort should be initiated early to identify and assess possible adversary course of action (COA) that could threaten friendly air mobility operations. Effective intelligence planning provides commanders at all levels with the intelligence they need to apply their available forces wisely, efficiently, and effectively. The 618 AOC (TACC) intelligence along with AMC A2 [Directorate of Intelligence] support operational level planning of all USTRANSCOM air mobility missions and coordinates with USTRANSCOM's Intelligence Directorate to fulfill collection and production requirements. In the JAOC, intelligence professionals are integrated into the AMD to support mobility planning and execution with support from the JAOC intelligence, surveillance, and reconnaissance division to ensure AMD intelligence analysis and information is current and consistent.

See JP 2-0, Joint Intelligence, *for more information regarding the criticality of intelligence support.*

4. Vulnerabilities and Threats

a. **Vulnerabilities.** Air mobility forces are vulnerable to attack during all phases of theater and international flight operations, at home station, APOEs, en route locations, APODs, and forward airfields. Mission planning must include a thorough analysis of vulnerabilities requirements throughout all phases of flight and ground operations. Military and CRAF flights into civilian airfields and off-base billeting of aircrews create unique vulnerabilities that must be addressed with local policy authorities. Force protection specialists will work to ensure that all air mobility vulnerabilities are considered.

See JP 3-10, Joint Security Operations in Theater, *for additional information on force protection in a theater of operations.*

b. **Threats.** Air mobility planning must begin with threat analysis and threat avoidance. Normally, mobility assets operate in a permissive to low-threat environment. Threat mitigation in the OA may require significant integration with joint/coalition air and ground combat forces for force protection during planning and execution. Planners must address the unique aspects of airborne, ground, electromagnetic, CBRN, and medical threats to air mobility operations.

(1) **Airborne Threats.** Air mobility aircraft are vulnerable to surface-to-surface, surface-to-air, and air-to-air threats. Large fixed-wing air mobility assets have significant radar signatures and lack maneuverability, fly slower speeds, and in many instances are equipped with limited or onboard defensive systems. The smaller fixed wing airlift aircraft and helicopters have lower radar cross sections; however, they suffer equally with limited onboard defensive systems. Both large and small aircraft are vulnerable to CBRN contamination, though aircrews are trained to survive and operate in such environments.

(2) **Ground Threats.** Air mobility aircraft, aircrews, and support personnel are particularly vulnerable during ground activities. On/offload operations offer large, stationary targets for adversary direct-fire and stand-off weapons. Commanders and their staffs should consider the employment of expedited ground operations (e.g., engine-running offload and combat offload/onload) to reduce vulnerability to ground threats. Perimeter and other

United States Air Force C-17 aircraft dispensing flares.

security measures should be planned and coordinated with those responsible for the area outside the base/airfield compound (e.g., joint security area coordinator).

(3) **Electronic Warfare (EW) Threats.** Air mobility operations are increasingly threatened by emerging EW capabilities. Aircrews must plan to use alternative procedures to overcome communications and Global Positioning System (GPS) jamming capabilities. Adversaries may attempt to employ EW to disrupt airfield operations at APODs.

(4) **CBRN Threat.** CBRN threats include the capability to employ and the intentional employment of, or intent to employ, weapons or improvised devices to produce CBRN hazards. Adversary use of CBRN weapons against air mobility forces represents a significant threat. Although aircrews are trained and equipped to operate in a contaminated environment, the contamination of airlift aircraft may limit options for the deployment, sustainment, and redeployment of forces. The JFC must take every precaution available to prevent the contamination of air mobility aircraft and develop plans to decontaminate aircraft which may become compromised.

(5) **Emergence of Pandemic Disease.** Regional endemic diseases are characterized by high human-to-human transmissibility and rapid onset of severe morbidity. When an endemic disease becomes pandemic, it threatens military readiness and imposes significant constraints on global air mobility operations. Although the Department of State (DOS) has a shelter-in-place policy for infected overseas areas, civil disturbance or political instability may necessitate a noncombatant evacuation operation (NEO) of noninfected individuals from areas abroad experiencing outbreaks. DOD will support the NEO with USTRANSCOM assets when directed by SecDef to do so. DOD movement of contagious

patients requires approval of the GCCs, CDRUSTRANSCOM, and SecDef in consultation with medical authorities. To prevent the spread of disease, the JFC will institute passenger screening measures. Patients with known or suspected highly contagious diseases should receive treatment in place.

c. **Threat Avoidance and Mitigation**

(1) Ideally, threat avoidance is the preferred defensive tactic for mobility aircraft. Threat avoidance tactics include over-flight, alternate routing, operating at night or in adverse weather, and using EZ operations. Since not all mobility aircraft, especially tankers, possess warning and defensive systems, they must depend upon combat air patrol and SEAD assets for protection and threat warnings. While mobility aircraft can reduce risk through threat-avoidance tactics, commanders should consider the lack of defensive countermeasures and perform proper operational risk management prior to operating air mobility aircraft in non-permissive environments. This limitation can reduce air mobility assets' flexibility to support national policy across the range of military operations and should be considered by planners of both combat and combat support missions. Therefore, using the most up-to-date intelligence from the JFC to identify potential threat locations is key to mission planning.

(2) When avoidance is not possible, threat mitigation is the next preferred option. Planners can mitigate the threat to mobility aircraft by using a variety of active and passive measures. Active protective measures include fighter escort, ground support forces employing measures that deny potential threats from interdicting air routes, antiaircraft defenses, ballistic missile defenses and tactical lasers for airfield defense, and SEAD. Passive measures include such things as air base defense, route and altitude selection, reduced ground times, dispersed aircraft basing operating at night or in adverse weather, and self-defense systems including the use of onboard warning receivers, flare/chafe dispensers, and CBRN detection devices. For CBRN hazards it may not be possible to avoid aircraft contamination, especially if the mission is critical. Some measures to mitigate the effects of CBRN hazards include limiting the retrograde of contaminated cargo to "mission critical" cargo, and identification of a theater decontamination strategy for air mobility aircraft. The Services do not have the capability to conduct clearance decontamination, therefore, once an aircraft is contaminated, its utility will be restricted.

(3) **OPSEC.** Conduct mission planning to heighten uncertainty by potential threat elements concerning the location, timing, and avenues of approach. This includes employing OPSEC procedures to deny knowledge of schedules, routes, departure points, and arrival location and times. Planners should also consider employing deception when conducting operations in high or unknown threat environments to confuse potential adversaries about the route, timing and location of air mobility operations.

5. **Communications Systems**

a. **Communication planning** integrates the communications capabilities of joint force components. These plans should include en route communications procedures and automated information systems to support movement reporting; call words or call signs, frequencies, communications equipment, and supplies to be delivered; the sequence of their delivery; and code words for significant events.

b. The most appropriate component will have responsibility for the following functions:

(1) Communications-electronics during air movement/aerial refueling.

(2) Develop and maintain a communications net for early operations in the objective area.

(3) Develop and maintain a communications net between the departure airfield and LZ (or arrival airfield) for air land operations.

(4) Secure rapid and reliable communications from the objective area through the communications and computer systems of geographic combatant commands and other headquarters immediately upon the arrival of airlift personnel; communications from the joint force headquarters to and between component commands; and from DOS or other agencies in the objective area.

(5) Formulate, publish, and distribute the communications-electronics operating instructions and joint communications-electronics operating instructions.

(6) Relay-type communications for disseminating intelligence or mission changes to the airborne force commanders while they are en route to the objective area.

(7) Jamming operations and coordination to prevent interference with friendly C2.

c. Various computer and communications systems along with their associated databases and peripheral equipment are included as elements of GAMSS and are used when planning and executing air mobility operations. Use of these systems for air mobility operations is highly encouraged to facilitate the flow of critical information between operational components. These include but are not limited to:

(1) **APEX System.** A system of joint policies, procedures, and reporting structures, supported by communications and computer systems, that is used by the JPEC to monitor, plan, and execute mobilization, deployment, employment, sustainment, redeployment, and demobilization activities associated with joint operations.

(2) **Global Air Transportation Execution System (GATES).** GATES is AMC's aerial port operations and management information system designed to support automated cargo and passenger processing, reporting of in transit visibility data to IGC, and billing to AMC's financial management directorate.

(3) **Global C2 System.** Highly mobile, deployable C2 system supporting forces for joint and multinational operations across the range of military operations, anytime and anywhere in the world with compatible, interoperable, and integrated command, control, communications, computers, and intelligence systems.

(4) **Consolidated Air Mobility Planning System (CAMPS).** CAMPS provides air mobility mission planners with an integrated view for airlift and AR requirements management, planning, and scheduling of AMC/MAF air mobility resources to support peacetime, contingency, humanitarian, and wartime operations. It also provides advanced user capabilities for operational planning and allocation management for AR missions, SAAMs, and GCC airlift requirements.

(5) **Global Decision Support System (GDSS).** As the primary C2 system for AMC's airlift and AR missions, GDSS provides aircraft schedules, arrival and/or departure, and aircraft status data to support ITV of aircraft and aircrews.

(6) **High-Frequency Global Communications System.** A global, high power, communications system providing beyond line-of-sight connectivity to GAMSS forces world-wide. This includes ITV, tactical data links, weather information, threat warnings, nuclear C2 messaging, and other secure voice and data services.

(7) **Joint Enterprise Network Manager (JENM).** JENM is an enterprise network planner and management tool used to support end-to-end services and connections to the DOD information networks. This tool supports the nework architecture from a Joint communication plan allowing for network connectivity across Service and geographical lines using internet protocol-based tactical waveforms (e.g., Wideband Networking Waveform, Soldier Radio Waveform, and Mobile User Objective System).

Additional information concerning communication system planning can be found in JP 6-0, Joint Communications System.

6. Sustainment

Operations and logistics are most effectively integrated as part of a collaborative planning process that includes subordinate component commands, supporting commands, and global providers. Equally important with planning is the active integration of sustainment movements from point of origin to point of need to ensure seamless delivery and retrograde of sustainment cargo. USTRANSCOM develops integrated distribution route structures based on the needs of the CCDRs to ensure timely performance through all segments of the joint distribution pipeline.

a. Historically, demand for items increases faster than the supply system can provide, and special management actions might become necessary. Anticipating the demand for sustainment movements requires a shared situational awareness and close collaboration between staffs during development of future plans and future operations concepts. Sustainment movements are usually a combination of push and pull resupply that requires a flexible means of modulating airlift capacity to respond to varying demand patterns and TDD parameters.

b. A key consideration during sustainment planning is the modal balance between airlift and surface movements. USTRANSCOM supports routine sustainment operations through scheduled airlift operations such as channel service and scheduled sealift via commercial liner service. Levels of transportation service for sustainment movements are often predicated on rules and transportation priorities applied during requisition or acquisition of supplies, which includes air clearance authority processes established by each service. However, there is no substitute for active planning to ensure sustainment movements are supported with the appropriate transportation mode to efficiently meet the needs of the CCDRs, Service components, and other supported organizations.

c. Routine sustainment planning usually assumes that user requirements and general air and ground security situations allow some flexibility in the actual delivery times of specific loads.

d. Combat sustainment operations reinforce or resupply units engaged in combat, and permit timely return of reparable parts, often in critically short supply, to designated repair points. Once delivered to the combat zone, an inserted force may be totally dependent upon subsequent airlift operations for sustainment, movement, withdrawal, redeployment, or AE of casualties. Combat sustainment planning usually assumes that operational requirements and assessed threats allow little or no flexibility in the delivery times, locations, and load configurations. Combat requirements and cargo handling limitations at forward operating locations drive flight schedules and determine whether palletized cargo can be handled effectively. Operational effectiveness is the primary objective, and the efficient use of aircraft and support resources is secondary.

e. Sustainment should be planned to utilize backhaul capacity. Depending on theater and user priorities, typical backhaul loads might include redeploying forces, friendly evacuees, detainees, and excess or repairable material. However, reset and reconstitution of military forces may drive scheduled retrograde movements with the same operational urgency and TDD objectives as other sustainment movements.

Additional information concerning sustainment can be found in JP 4-0, Joint Logistics, *and JP 4-09,* Distribution Operations.

7. **Assessment**

Assessments must be conducted prior to and during air mobility operations.

a. Prior to executing air mobility operations, consideration must be given to the following planning factors:

(1) Airfields, to include capabilities and limitations and airland facilities available in the departure and arrival areas must be assessed, particularly those in underdeveloped countries where their status may be questionable. Mobility planners should consider runway characteristics as well as taxiway, parking, ramp, and cargo handling areas for operational suitability, and determination of maximum (aircraft) on ground (MOG). Additionally, planners should consider establishing a regional air movement control center (RAMCC) to coordinate movements of civilian fixed-wing airlift in support of coalition military, humanitarian, and commercial air operations throughout the designated AOR by assigning arrival and departure times at selected airfields in the AOR and coordinating over flights. Arrival slot time coordination between the RAMCC and airlift control team ensures the

MOG is not exceeded. Preplanned aircraft arrival slot times avoid ramp congestion and foster the synergistic effect of the entire rapid global air mobility force.

Additional information concerning RAMCC procedures can be found in Air Force Doctrine Document (AFDD) 3-52, Airspace Control.

(2) An airfield's infrastructure also impacts the support GAMSS/JTF-PO forces can provide to the air mobility flow. The hours of operation, climatology, weather services, flight planning support, airfield lighting systems, airfield navigational aids, communications, marshalling/storage areas, and road networks are all requirements that need consideration during planning phases.

(3) Host-nation support (HNS) capability and willingness is a critical consideration in the planning phase. HNS can include diplomatic clearances, airspace access, lodging, food services, water, communications, labor, local transportation, or other types of support.

(4) Availability of fuel at support locations may limit air mobility support. POL planning/requirements should include the amount needed for aircraft and ground equipment. Planners should consider POL storage capacity, fueling system condition and type, dispense rates, as well as POL acquisition, either from the HN or by resupply. Aircraft fuel is usually a major limiting factor and should therefore be the primary focus. At austere locations, aerial refueling can lessen the effects of shortages in ground refueling capabilities.

b. Assessments must be conducted continuously during air mobility operations. Assessors must ensure that the user's requirement is being met IAW established priorities and air mobility forces are being used efficiently and adapting to changes in the operations tempo or focus. Evaluation tools must include metrics to determine on-time delivery amount of cargo/fuel on- or off-loaded and airdrop delivery precision.

c. Continuous operational assessment that links operational objectives to airlift tasks is the key to ensuring effective employment of air mobility assets. At the same time, economy of force in air mobility operations has a global impact. USTRANSCOM and the MAF in general support all Services' and government agencies' operational requirements simultaneously with a finite force to effectively meet the highest priority air mobility needs. Effectiveness is paramount, but economy of force in planning and execution is an essential consideration.

Additional information concerning assessment factors associated with air mobility operation planning can be found in JP 3-0, Joint Operations.

8. Multinational Planning Considerations

a. The joint planner should consider complementary multinational capabilities during COA development. However, this capability should be balanced against the potential for competition for US transportation assets to deliver those multinational units into the theater.

b. In planning for multinational operations, the joint planner should be aware of the legal considerations in providing or receiving logistics support from multinational partners.

The Foreign Assistance Act, the Arms Export Control Act, acquisition and cross-servicing agreement authority, the Federal Property and Administrative Services Act of 1949 (as amended), the Fly America Act, and the Cargo Preference Acts all address the degree of support that the US can provide to or receive from other nations. In addition, specific legislative language contained in DOD authorization or appropriation acts may limit US ability to receive and/or provide logistic support from and/or to allies. The joint planner should include the legal advisor in all stages of multinational operations planning and execution for legal compliance.

c. The legal considerations of multinational support notwithstanding, air operations are an integral part of most multinational planning efforts. The multinational force air component commander is responsible for air operations planning and develops a concept for integrating air operations capabilities. US component commanders and multinational force commanders should provide highly trained liaison staffs to facilitate integration, coordination, and synchronization of air operations. Air planning should also include the use of logistic air assets and airfields. It is important to ensure that all planners understand the capabilities and limitations that each country brings to the fight. In the event that no established multinational guidance is available, planning considerations for multinational air operations should resemble those for joint operations.

For additional information, refer to JP 3-16, Multinational Operations.

9. Other Planning Factors

a. **Materiel Collection and Classification Planning.** Because much abandoned or captured materiel or contaminated equipment may be usable by friendly forces, ground and air commanders should develop plans for their retrograde, consistent with the urgency and length of the primary mission.

b. **Planning for Detainees.** Detainee collection points should be located near air terminal facilities to aid in air evacuation, but not so close that they are endangered by possible adversary targeting.

For additional information, see JP 3-63, Detainee Operations.

c. **Medical Support Planning.** A complete medical estimate is usually conducted for each phase of an operation. The respective Service component medical planners should conduct detailed medical supply planning and medical support operations. Plans should allow for probable losses of medical equipment and supplies during delivery into the objective area. Estimates should be made for replacement items to cover losses due to battle actions, evacuation of patients, and other causes. The evacuating medical activity usually provides litters, blankets, splints, and other medical items accompanying patients during evacuation. Planners responsible for AE should ensure plans address the potential requirement to move CBRN contaminated patients IAW DOD and USTRANSCOM policy.

Additional information regarding medical support planning can be found in JP 4-02, Health Services.

d. **AE**

(1) **Responsibilities.** AE refers to TS en route care of regulated patients to and between MTFs, using organic and/or contracted aircraft with medical aircrew trained explicitly for this mission. AE forces can operate as far forward as aircraft are able to conduct air operations, across the full range of military operations, and in all operating environments. Specialty medical teams may be assigned to work with the AE aircrew to support patients requiring more intensive en route care.

Information on the AE mission, Service component and common-user systems, organizations, and C2 procedures is contained in JP 4-02, Health Services.

(2) **Common-User System.** USTRANSCOM and GCCs perform common-user AE with available air mobility assets. Patient movements are managed through the USTRANSCOM Regulating and C2 Evacuation System. Normally, patients are evacuated from theater hospitalization to OCONUS definitive care facilities and then on to CONUS definitive care facilities. Movement within and from forward resuscitative care capability is normally a Service component responsibility; however, operations that incorporate use of theater hospitalization capability MTFs may require casualty movement from forward resuscitative care capability and evacuation to theater hospitalization capability by the joint AE common-user system. However, in selected circumstances, airlift can be apportioned to evacuate patients from as far forward in a theater as the aircraft can operate. Far forward intratheater and intertheater patient movement operations will be coordinated through the JAOC/AOC.

e. **Weather.** The anticipation of weather effects on operations mitigated through planning provides invaluable dividends in efficiencies on strategic mobility. Incorporation of weather considerations into mission planning is essential to mitigate risk, identify opportunity, select ideal environmental conditions, and to optimize routing and DZ/LZ selection. Planning for weather considerations is accomplished in the AOC at the operational level.

Information on integrating weather considerations into planning is contained in JP 3-59, Meteorological and Oceanographic Operations.

f. **Withdrawal or Restaging Plan.** The withdrawal or restaging of forces by air should be done IAW the general guidelines for redeployment and extraction airlift operations.

(1) Other specific considerations that may be important to the success of these operations include the local air superiority situation and the possible need for friendly deception. Such operations should mask these withdrawal movements for as long as possible. Clearly, **the likelihood of success will be increased by conducting these operations early enough to allow for comprehensive planning and organized execution.** Once the appropriate ground force commander orders an operation and establishes movement priorities, load plans, and departure points, **the COMAFFOR or JFACC (if designated) should control the air movement.** GAMSS units should be placed at the departure points, if possible.

(2) **The ground force commander should provide trained loading teams at the departure points to assist airfield support units** in loading and securing equipment, with technical assistance and supervision from USAF personnel. Specific withdrawal and equipment destruction procedures are contained in appropriate Service manuals.

g. **Space Support Planning.** Friendly space-based capabilities can greatly enhance any air mobility operation. In general, space-based capabilities such as GPS signals and satellite communications (SATCOM) are readily available for use by friendly forces without needing to be requested. However, planners should be aware of possible constraints on space-based capabilities and should also assess their need for tailored space capabilities which must be requested prior to mission execution.

(1) **Constraints.** Availability of space-based capabilities can be constrained by many factors including the space environment and enemy activity. Planners should consult their weather office for environmental factors which could cause signal interference or anomalies. Additionally, planners should request intelligence assessments of enemy capability to disrupt friendly space capabilities and plan accordingly. This includes enemy jamming of GPS and SATCOM signals.

(2) **Tailored Capabilities.** Tailored space capabilities can provide additional resources toward mission success. Often times these capabilities require intensive planning prior to mission execution and should be requested as early in the mission planning process as possible.

h. **Information Operations (IO) Planning.** IO are integral to the successful planning and execution of air mobility operations. IO planning in support of global air mobility operations is conducted by the AFTRANS staff in support of the 618 AOC (TACC). IO can support both offensive and defensive operations simultaneously, but mobility operations focus is primarily on defensive operations while deconflicting theater offensive operations planning. IO planning requires early and detailed JIPOE and must be an integral part of, not an addition to, the overall planning effort.

(1) **EW.** EW threat planning is critical to airlift operations. The threat of directed energy (e.g., lasers and high-power microwave) weapons as well as the adversary's infrared and traditional electronic attack radio frequency energy capabilities to MAF operations is increasing in sophistication and effectiveness at an accelerating rate. Mobility forces also require enhanced situational awareness, force protection, reduced radar cross section, and defensive systems to survive in the electromagnetic environment. Effective countermeasures such as flare based defensive systems and large aircraft infrared countermeasures reduce the lethality of threats encountered when avoidance is not possible or unknown. The MAF generally accepts aircraft arrivals and departures to be in the "public domain" and are concerned with probable/likely threat in the vicinity of airfields.

(2) **Information Assurance.** Based on mission classification, the MAF conducts mission planning on both classified and unclassified C2 systems using the SECRET Internet Protocol Router Network (SIPRNET) and Nonsecure Internet Protocol Router Network (NIPRNET). Because adversaries attack our information sources and information systems at

multiple locations simultaneously, information assurance actions are essential. The MAF must ensure Service components comply with established USSTRATCOM cyberspace policy and guidance to provide well-defined boundaries with protection mechanisms (e.g., firewalls, system interoperability solutions, data management zones, and intrusion detection and protection systems) that monitor and detect unauthorized internal and external activity.

(3) **Military Deception (MILDEC).** MILDEC planning and execution is used to deliberately mislead adversary decision makers as to air mobility capabilities, intentions, and operations, thereby causing the adversary to take specific actions (or inactions) that will contribute to the accomplishment of the mission.

(4) **OPSEC.** OPSEC denies the adversary information required to correctly assess friendly capabilities and intentions. AMC's OPSEC planning identifies critical information to determine if air mobility plans can be observed by adversary intelligence systems. Once critical information has been identified, (such as for protection reasons, force composition, movement and refueling schedules, troop and equipment), then security measures and procedures are executed to eliminate or reduce adversary exploitation. Unlike other security programs that seek to protect classified information, OPSEC measures identify, control, and protect generally unclassified mobility operations mission profiles and signatures associated with sensitive operations and activities.

(5) **MILDEC and OPSEC.** Working in tandem, MILDEC and OPSEC complement each other. Controlling the adversary's access to information by denying or permitting access to specific information can shape adversaries' perceptions. Through the vulnerabilities identified by OPSEC, MILDEC seeks to encourage incorrect analysis, causing the adversary to arrive at specific false deductions, while OPSEC seeks to deny real information to an adversary, and prevent correct deduction of friendly plans. OPSEC planning in support of the deception plan is just as important as OPSEC of the real plan, since compromise of the deception may expose the real plan. MILDEC can directly support the OPSEC plan by creating numerous false signatures and indicators. The intent is to manipulate indicators which give insight into operations. Signatures should be managed and adjusted to produce the planned effect. Air mobility operations must protect mission critical information identified by the supported commander for both airlift and AR operations. Appropriate deception or misinformation plans, developed early in the planning stages, may help conceal or divert attention from aircraft and troop movements. However, these plans should not jeopardize alternate plans or other operations within the area.

See JP 3-13, Information Operations, *for more detail regarding information operations support of air mobility operations.*

i. **Public Affairs (PA).** For air mobility operations, PA planners predict the level of public and media interest and develop PA guidance that best meets the information needs of the public and is in line with strategic guidance and operational objectives without compromising OPSEC or information security. PA and other information-related capabilities can shape and influence theater HN/indigenous population perceptions within the OA. For air mobility operations, the use of information-related capabilities can help minimize the adverse effects of inaccurate information and analysis, violations of OPSEC, and the spread of disinformation and misinformation that could otherwise threaten US and multinational efforts.

j. **Special Technical Operations (STO) Planning.** The AFTRANS or JAOC STO cell is responsible for integrating STO capabilities in direct support of mobility operations during deployment and redeployment. The AFTRANS STO cell coordinates with appropriate JAOC STO cells and capability providers to ensure planning and execution of STO capabilities. The JAOC STO cell is integrated into the JAOC divisions to develop the required classified annexes for STO capabilities. Effective support for the JFC's mobility requirements demands air mobility experts are integrated into the STO and that STO cell representatives understand and develop support plans to enhance mobility operations.

Intentionally Blank

CHAPTER IV
AIRLIFT

> *"Air power must be more than force because the problems of the world must increasingly be addressed by the military with more than force. Many of the crises and conflicts in our shrinking world are no longer highly susceptible to resolution through the projection of force, but—as in protection of the Kurds in the wake of Operation DESERT STORM—will require the projection of infrastructures such as security, medical care, communications, and transportation."*
>
> **Carl Builder, The Icarus Syndrome, 1993**

1. General

a. **Airlift operations transport and deliver forces and materiel through the air in support of strategic, operational, and/or tactical objectives.** Airlift offers its customers a high degree of speed, range, and flexibility. Airlift enables commanders to respond and operate in a wide variety of circumstances and time frames that would be impractical through other modes of transportation.

b. Airlift supports the US National Military Strategy by rapidly transporting personnel and materiel to and from or within a theater. **Airlift is a cornerstone of global force projection.** It provides the means to rapidly deploy and redeploy forces, on short notice, to any location worldwide. Within a theater, airlift employment missions can be used to transport forces directly into combat. To maintain a force's level of effectiveness, airlift sustainment missions provide resupply of equipment, personnel, and supplies. Finally, airlift supports the movement of patients to treatment facilities and noncombatants to safe havens. Airlift's characteristics—speed, flexibility, range, and responsiveness—complement other US mobility assets.

2. Airlift Operations

Airlift operations are defined by the nature of the mission rather than the airframe used. Most aircraft are not exclusively assigned to one operational classification. In fact, the vast majority of the air mobility force is capable of accomplishing any classification of airlift. Intertheater and intratheater capabilities are available to all users of USAF airlift.

a. **Intertheater Airlift.** Intertheater airlift provides the critical link between theaters.

(1) During deployment operations, intertheater airlift requirements, while significant, are to a large degree predictable. Such requirements normally are identified in the TPFDD associated with a particular operation plan (OPLAN) or OPORD. A TPFDD can be tailored to meet specific requirements when the mission is not aligned with an OPLAN or modified to meet the requirements associated with a particular COA. Time-definite resupply via airlift from CONUS to the theaters is critical in maintaining the flow of materiel

necessary to sustain operations. This concept uses both military and commercial aircraft to support the sustainment flow that must begin as soon as deployment operations begin.

(2) **A key strength of airlift is its ability to quickly redploy forces from one theater to another.** Airlift enables commanders to rapidly reposition forces between theaters, thereby deterring potential aggressors from acting when US forces are engaged elsewhere.

(3) Diplomatic overflight and landing clearances are key to establishing an efficient air bridge for deployment of TPFDD forces and sustainment. En route aircraft clearances may be denied to aircraft suspected of having been contaminated. The diplomatic clearances are to be done IAW DOD Directive 4500.54E, *DOD Foreign Clearance Program (FCP)*. The JFC must anticipate that formerly contaminated aircraft may be removed from intertheater airlift operations.

HUMANITARIAN RELIEF OPERATION: TSUNAMI SUPPORT

On 26 December 2004 an undersea earthquake struck the Indian Ocean, triggering a series of devastating tsunamis along the coasts of most bordering landmasses. With waves up to 100 feet, the tsunami killed more than 225,000 people in eleven countries, and inundated coastal communities. It was one of the deadliest natural disasters in history.

The plight of the many affected people and countries prompted a widespread humanitarian response. In all, the worldwide community donated more than $7 billion (2004 US dollars) in humanitarian aid, which was needed because of widespread damage of the infrastructure, shortages of food and water, and economic damage. Epidemics were of special concern due to the high population density and tropical climate of the affected areas. The main focus of humanitarian and government agencies was to provide sanitation facilities and fresh drinking water to contain the spread of diseases such as cholera, diphtheria, dysentery, typhoid and hepatitis. There was also a great concern that the death toll could increase as disease and hunger spread. However, because of the initial quick response, this was minimized.

Operation UNIFIED ASSISTANCE, controlled by Combined Support Force (CSF) 536, delivered 6,685 passengers, 5,444 cargo tons of relief supplies and medical aid. With a focus on air mobility as opposed to combat operations, CSF 536 showcased how Air Mobility contributes to humanitarian relief operations as part of a multinational effort that included nongovernmental organizations.

Brigadier General Jouas, US Air Force,
Director, Air Component Coordination Element,
Operation UNIFIED ASSISTANCE

---

b. **Intratheater Airlift.** Intratheater airlift provides air movement of forces, personnel, and materiel within a GCC's AOR. Typically, aircraft capable of accomplishing a wide range of operational and tactical level missions conduct these operations. Intratheater operations provide both general support, usually through common-user airlift in response to the JFC's movement priorities, and direct support, normally using Service-organic airlift assets or with assets provided by another Service to responsively satisfy Service component commander's priorities. Intratheater airlift requirements include TPFDD force movements and the continuation of sustainment movements arriving in the theater, as well as on-demand movements and routinely scheduled airlift missions for the movement of non-unit related cargo and personnel.

(1) Unit movements within the theater are in response to the JFC's operation or campaign plan. Once combat units are deployed to a theater, the JFC may use intratheater airlift to maneuver forces to exploit weaknesses in the adversary's position. In this capacity, airlift allows the JFC to reposition forces expeditiously, achieve surprise, and control the timing and tempo of operations.

(2) Movements within a theater also permit the continuing resupply of forward units. These requirements normally are predictable, regular, and quantifiable when the forces are not engaged in combat operations. During pre- or post-hostilities, these requirements can usually be fulfilled through a fixed resupply schedule. However, once forces are engaged, resupply requirements increase dramatically and become more unpredictable and variable. The ability of airlift to rapidly and flexibly accommodate the critical resupply requirements of units engaged and operating in such a dynamic environment provides commanders with an essential warfighting capability.

3. Airlift Missions

The basic mission of airlift is passenger and cargo movement. This includes combat employment and sustainment, AE, special operations support, and operational support airlift (OSA). USAF airlift forces perform these missions to achieve strategic-, operational-, and tactical-level objectives across the range of military operations. Normally, movement requirements are fulfilled through regularly scheduled channel missions over fixed route structures with personnel and cargo capacity available to all customers. These regularly scheduled requirements are validated through the appropriate Service organization to USTRANSCOM or GCC, and then tasked by the 618 AOC (TACC), an AMD, or another appropriate C2 node. Depending on user requirements, requests not supportable through the channel structure can be fulfilled through use of other mission categories such as SAAM, exercise, and contingency missions. Requests that cannot be satisfied by any of the above missions may be referred to other transportation modes of the DTS. The airlift system has the flexibility to surge and meet requirements that exceed routine, peacetime demands for passenger and cargo movement. For example, during Operation ENDURING FREEDOM (OEF) and Operation IRAQI FREEDOM (OIF), new channel routes and structures were established to support the significantly increased airlift demands.

a. **Combat Employment and Sustainment. Combat airlift missions are missions that rapidly move forces, equipment and supplies from one area to another in response**

to changing battle conditions. Combat employment missions allow a commander to insert surface forces directly and quickly into battle and to sustain combat operations. For example, combat missions may involve airdropping paratroopers behind adversary lines. Combat sustainment missions may consist of reinforcement of front-line forces engaged with the adversary. Airlift affords commanders a high degree of combat maneuverability permitting them to bypass adversary troop strongholds. This provides friendly forces a potent offensive advantage and complicates the adversary's defensive preparations. The combat employment and sustainment mission usually accounts for a small percentage of total airlift sorties; nevertheless, its importance is far greater than the number of sorties indicates. This is a capability which, in most circumstances, cannot be accomplished by other means.

(1) While this mission provides significant capabilities, it also carries substantial risk. Success in combat and combat support hinges on air superiority and threat avoidance. This requires accurate and timely intelligence regarding threats along the ingress and egress routes and over the target area. Once delivered to the target area, the inserted force may be totally dependent upon subsequent airlift operations for sustainment, movement, withdrawal, or redeployment.

(2) Another important aspect of combat employment and sustainment is the concept of **forcible entry.** In performing this mission, airlift forces are usually matched with airborne, air assault, light infantry, or special forces specifically designed for delivery by air. This mission normally involves inserting airborne forces via airdrop; however, carefully planned airland assault operations can be equally effective. An example of intertheater forcible entry operations is the airdrop capability that the USAF provides for the Army. For more information, see JP 3-18, *Joint Forcible Entry Operations*.

(3) **Deployment and Sustainment in Nonlinear Operations.** In nonlinear operations, forces orient on objectives without geographic reference to adjacent forces. These operations require significant airlift/aerial delivery support for each deployment and continued sustainment. Nonlinear operations were applied during Operation JUST CAUSE. The joint forces oriented more on their assigned objectives (e.g., destroying an enemy force or seizing and controlling critical terrain or population centers) and less on their geographic relationship to other friendly forces. Nonlinear operations place a premium on air mobility.

b. **AE.** AE is the movement of regulated patients under medical supervision to and between MTFs by air transportation. AE specifically refers to USAF provided movement of regulated patients using organic and/or contracted mobility airframes with AE aircrew trained explicitly for this mission. Movement of patients requires special ATC considerations to comply with patient-driven altitude and pressurization restrictions as well as medical equipment approved for use with aircraft systems. Several processes occur once validated PMRs have been identified.

(1) The aeromedical evacuation control team (AECT) within each theater's JAOC/AOC performs AE operational mission planning, tasking, and scheduling of airlift and AE assets to support patient movement for intratheater missions. The AETC responds to PMRs that have been validated by the PMRC.

FLEXIBILITY IS THE KEY TO AIR POWER

When Princess Patricia's Light Infantry Regiment, a Canadian unit with 850 troops and 1500 tons of equipment, redeployed from Kandahar following their tour supporting Operation ENDURING FREEDOM in 2002, United States Transportation Command (USTRANSCOM) determined airlift was the best mode available. The Air Mobility Command (AMC) had several options, including what type of aircraft to use and the route they would fly. In the end, C-5s were used in a stage operation out of Diego Garcia in the Indian Ocean. Five C-5s, six complete aircrews, 50 maintainers and aerial porters, and a staff were prepositioned at Diego Garcia. Because of the fuel requirement, the C-5s could not carry their maximum cargo loads and fly nonstop from Afghanistan to Diego, so an air refueling was planned en route. This allowed the C-5s to max out their cargo weight, which cut the number of aircraft and required sorties into Kandahar by half.

This operation highlights two key points: first, it shows the importance of the warfighter giving Commander, USTRANSCOM his requirements without insisting on a specific platform. Had C-17s been used, it would have required 45 sorties, as opposed to 28 C-5 sorties. The aircrews flew tactical arrivals and departures, and ground personnel conducted engine running onloads to minimize ground time in Kandahar- ground times were cut to as little as 25 minutes, vice the normal 3 hours, 15 minutes. Most of this time savings was due to eliminating the ground refueling requirement. Minimizing the number of aircraft and sorties maximizes safety in all cases, but it is especially important in combat zones.

The second point this operation highlighted was the fact that often it is better to use a supported/supporting command relationship. There are times when it's best to change operational control of aircraft to the warfighter, but many times it is best for him to pass his requirements to USTRANSCOM and let "Big AMC" draw from its entire air mobility fleet and utilize its vast command and control and planning resources to conduct the operation.

VARIOUS SOURCES

(2) For contingency or wartime operations, the AECT provides AE C2 for assigned AE forces. The AECT is the source of AE operational expertise within the AMD. The AECT will coordinate AE operational mission planning, tasking, and scheduling of airlift and AE assets to support patient movement in coordination with the PMRC. The AECT will work closely with other AOC divisions and teams to ensure AE missions are completely integrated into the ATO.

(3) Intertheater AE will be typically OPCON to USTRANSCOM with C2 provided by the 618 AOC (TACC)and is accomplished using designated or retrograde organic AE aircraft. If AE and airlift planners anticipate that PMRs will exceed organic capabilities, CRAF may be activated. The number of CRAF AE activated depends on the number of

---

AEROMEDICAL EVACUATION SUCCESS STORY

The ability to use virtually any aircraft on-site or in-system (vice the old system of dedicated aeromedical evacuation (AE) aircraft) provided a quick response to casualty movement requirements. Air Mobility Command AE forces supported approximately 7,847 patient movements between 1January and 20 May 2004. "Some of the guys are hurt pretty bad (sic). I wish that I could help them somehow, but the most I can do is make sure the aircraft are configured right before every launch, make sure that there is always a crew that is ready to fly, and that the aircraft launches on time. You will never know how much it means to me that I have had the opportunity to participate."—Deployed AE support troop, in email home.

Air Mobility By The Numbers

---

organic aircraft available, the predicted number of patients requiring movement and the estimated length of the contingency. When CRAF AE capability is exceeded or on an urgent or priority basis, retrograde or dedicated AE aircraft may be used. Alternatives to CRAF AE or military aircraft may be pursued when competing airlift or evacuee requirements reduce airframe availability. These alternatives could include use of other organic military airlift, CRAF passenger aircraft, or authorization for commercial travel for ambulatory patients who do not require in-flight supportive medical care.

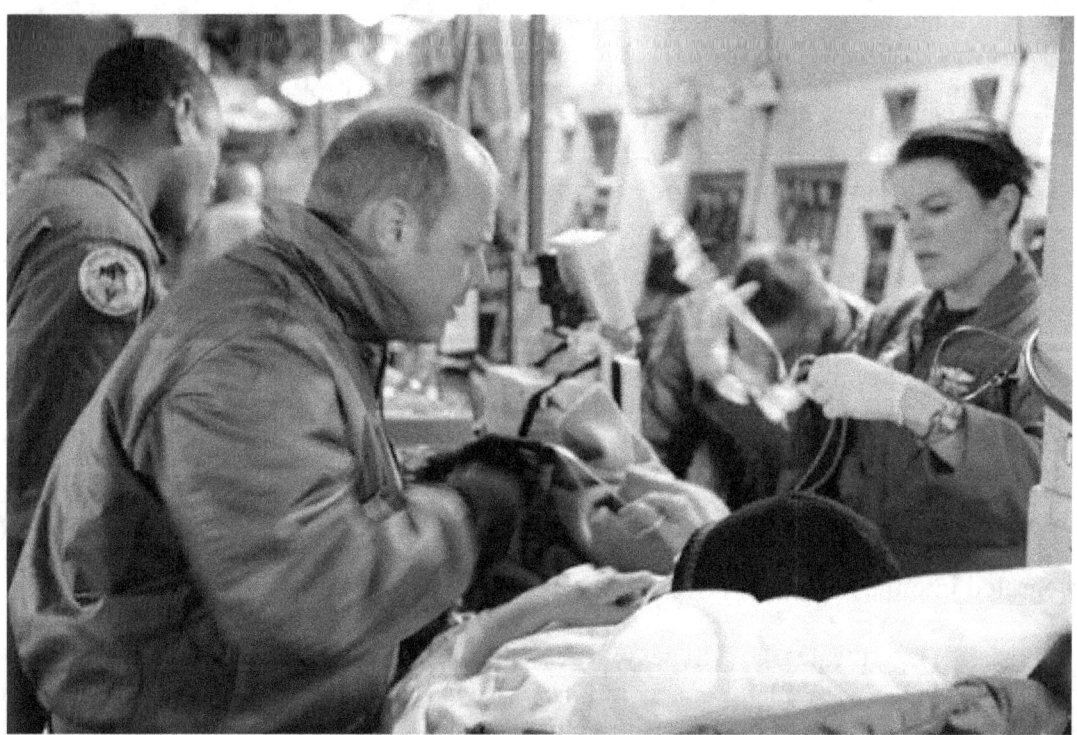

Aeromedical evacuation missions require use of medical equipment approved for use with aircraft systems.

A variety of operational support airlift aircraft illustrate the variety of airlift missions.

(4) Use of CRAF aircraft for AE will be dependent on the threat in the region. As civilian aircrews are neither trained nor equipped to fly in contaminated conditions, CRAF AE aircraft will not be used to move contaminated or contagious patients.

(5) Intratheater AE is the movement of casualties and/or patients within and/or out of the joint area of operations by fixed wing aircraft to theater hospitalization capability or definitive capability is generally accomplished using dedicated, designated, opportune, or scheduled aircraft. Intratheater assigned AE forces will be OPCON to the GCC with C2 provided by the GCC's AOC to provide ITV of patient movements and a handoff to the 618 AOC (TACC) for intertheater lift using designated or retrograde organic AE aircraft.

Further information on AE patient movement can be found in JP 4-02, Health Services; *AFTTP 3-3.AOC; and AFDD 3-17,* Air Mobility Operations and AFTTP 3-42.5, Aeromedical Evacuation.

c. **Special Operations Support.** Specified airlift forces provide unique airland and airdrop support to SOF. Since there are a limited number of airlift assets dedicated to this mission, the principle of economy of force is particularly applicable. When performing special operations missions, highly trained airlift and AR crews normally act as an integral member of a larger joint package. Because these airlift missions routinely operate under adverse conditions in a hostile environment, extensive planning, coordination, and training are required to enhance mission success. Airlift and AR used in a special operations role provides commanders the capability to achieve specific campaign objectives, which may not be attainable through more conventional airlift practices.

d. **OSA.** OSA is the movement of high-priority passengers and cargo with time, place, or mission-sensitive requirements. OSA missions are a special classification of airlift mission support to provide for the timely movement of limited numbers of priority personnel or cargo. The OSA aircraft fleet consists of executive and non-executive aircraft. The executive fleet is dedicated to the airlift of DOD and federal senior officials and DOD-approved senior officials. Non-executive aircraft support passenger and cargo airlift during peacetime, but also support CCMD wartime requirements during conflict. USTRANSCOM is responsible for the scheduling and tasking of OSA operations regarding CONUS-based assets while the Services validate OSA requests. Theaters with their own OSA fleets are responsible for scheduling and execution tasking of OSA operations within their AORs. Within a theater, OSA assets and their scheduling should reside with their respective Service component, and may be made available for tasking at the CCDRs direction.

Further information on OSA missions can be found in DOD Directive 4500.56, DOD Policy on the Use of Government Aircraft and Air Travel, *and DOD Instruction 4500.43,* Operational Support Airlift (OSA).

(1) In theory, almost any aircraft could contribute to the intratheater effort. In practice, however, the bulk of intratheater missions are normally done by fixed-wing aircraft provided by the USAF component, while some limited or specialized missions may be accomplished by fixed- and rotary-wing aircraft provided by other Services. It is important to consider that aircraft performance characteristics will be directly affected by such factors as gross weight, atmospheric conditions, runway length and condition, and flight obstacles as outlined in Service publications. Additionally, the Services operate more specialized fixed-wing transports capable of performing TS, mission-critical (MC) requirements for forward deployed units. TS/MC missions are those that are generally unplanned in nature and which respond to the supported commanders' immediate operational or tactical requirements.

(2) It is often difficult to view the relative contributions of the components of the joint force in isolation. Each is critical to the success of a joint operation and each has unique capabilities that cannot be duplicated. Common-user airlift achieves an economy of force. Rather than each Service and non-DOD agency providing its own airlift, airlift is consolidated and tasked to support all organizations. While different types of operations will have varying requirements, the following highlights some of the airlift requirements of the various organizations that use common-user airlift.

(a) **USTRANSCOM.** GAMSS forces normally deploy early in an operation to establish en route and destination support. This may consume a large portion of the first airlift missions.

(b) **Army.** Even though the Army has significant organic airlift assets, it often has the largest requirement for common-user airlift. ARFOR rely heavily on intertheater and intratheater airlift for deployment, airborne operations, and redeployment of personnel and early arriving or departing unit equipment. Sustainment is also moved during deployment, but its delivery must frequently be balanced against force deployment or redeployment requirements because these operations share the same deployment and distribution infrastructure and other resources. The Army's prepositioning program also requires significant airlift to move troops to designated locations to link up with prepositioned equipment.

(c) **Navy.** Sustainment and combat readiness of deployed naval forces depends on flexible and highly responsive intertheater airlift support. Afloat naval forces normally serve as a force enabler and consequently require the least amount of common-user airlift support. However, the Navy depends on common-user airlift to sustain forward-deployed operations with personnel, materiel, and mail from CONUS to overseas bases. The Navy depends on organic, land-based, fleet-essential airlift assets to transport passengers and cargo intratheater from the APOD to forward logistics sites for further transfer to fleet units. Naval organic airlift, known as Navy-unique fleet essential aircraft, then transports passengers, mail, and critical materiel from forward sites to underway forces. Although naval organic

Limited or specialized missions may be accomplished by fixed- and rotary-wing aircraft provided by Services other than the Air Force.

airlift satisfies most intratheater requirements, the Navy requires some common-user airlift to augment this capability.

(d) **Marine Corps.** Marine Corps forces require common-user airlift when deploying into a theater as part of either a maritime pre-positioning force MAGTF or as an air contingency MAGTF. During maritime pre-positioning force operations, Marine Corps forces are airlifted to join maritime pre-positioned equipment and supplies at the arrival and assembly area. Additional fly-in echelons of personnel, equipment, and supplies are airlifted into the theater to complete and sustain the force. The air contingency MAGTF requires intertheater airlift of both personnel and equipment. Depending on the mission, amphibious MAGTF operations ashore may require intertheater and intratheater common-user airlift support to sustain and/or support the force.

(e) **USAF.** Most USAF unit aircraft self-deploy; however, unit support personnel and equipment require airlift to the destination with or before the deploying unit aircraft. Dedication of significant airlift assets to USAF units may be required early in deployment operations. USAF units normally begin air operations shortly after arrival. Therefore, airlift must be able to rapidly deploy full squadron support packages, to include combat support elements, their equipment, and both initial and sustainment supplies.

(f) **Coast Guard.** Coast Guard operates a mixed fleet of fixed- and rotary-wing aircraft for organic airlift. It is able to provide flexible and responsive common-user airlift but is limited by statutory priorities and a lack of strategic support facilities. Its organic airlift is normally sufficient to satisfy Coast Guard airlift requirements. In addition, the Coast Guard often uses DOD airlift assistance for OCONUS deployments and CCMD-supported missions. Coast Guard common-user airlift is available to naval forces for wartime tasking. Non-wartime airlift may be requested from the Commander, Atlantic Area or the Commander, Pacific Area, under Title 31, United States Code (USC), Sections 1535 and 1536.

(g) **SOFs.** SOF have highly trained aircrews and specially configured aircraft dedicated to conduct specialized air mobility tasks including infiltration, exfiltration, and resupply of SOF. These aircraft are not part of the common-user system and have limited capability to perform large-scale deployment, sustainment, and redeployment operations. Due to their unique capabilities, special operations aircrew and aircraft may be requested to support other specific specialized air mobility missions, but must be deconflicted from higher priority special operations requirements. SOF are augmented by common-user airlift support. Additionally, selected conventional airlift forces with specially trained aircrews and modified aircraft may augment SOF airlift capability.

1. The JFSOCC obtains airlift and provides an STT to support airlift operations by following the procedures in this publication and in JP 3-05, *Special Operations*. Intratheater airlift forces provide valuable support for SOF. For routine logistics requirements, SOF request intratheater airlift support through their respective supporting Service component. When SOF units require airlift to perform special operations-specific missions that require specially trained and equipped airlift forces, they transmit their request through their SOF command channels. Airlift personnel (particularly aircrews) expected to provide employment airlift support to SOF, should be fully incorporated into the SOF operation planning process and, if necessary, entered into isolation for tactical rehearsals.

2. On the other hand, airlift aircraft and crews should not be taken out of the airlift system any longer than necessary to prepare them for the anticipated operation. Standing down aircraft for longer periods could waste valuable lift capacity and increase the signature of the SOF's preparation phase. Although it is possible for SOF to provide some common-user airlift to the theater if directed by the JFC, this would only be done in exceptional cases.

(h) **Contract Airlift.** National airlift policy dictates that commanders shift airlift workload to commercial carriers if surge and training requirements have been met and threat conditions allow. Gaining rapid access to commercial carriers through a flexible and responsive contractual mechanism is a significant force multiplier. Commercial carriers can provide tremendous capability using existing commercial networks on short notice allowing JFCs the flexibility to use organic aircraft for higher priority missions or for special missions unsuited for commercial airlift.

(i) **Other Non-DOD Agencies.** United States Government (USG) departments and agencies, such as the DOS and the Drug Enforcement Administration, use DOD airlift for activities such as NEO, counterdrug operations, foreign humanitarian assistance, and domestic support operations. Non-DOD agencies may use common-user airlift, providing the DOD mission is not impaired. The movement must be of an emergency, lifesaving nature, specifically authorized by statute, in direct support of the DOD mission, or requested by the head of an agency of the government under the Economy Act (Title 31, USC, Sections 1535 and 1536) and/or the Stafford Act. The Economy Act permits one federal agency to request the support of another, provided that, the requested services cannot be obtained more cheaply or conveniently by contract. Under this act, a lead federal agency may request the support of the DOD without a Presidential declaration of an emergency as required by the Stafford Act. The Stafford Disaster Relief and Emergency Assistance Act sets the policy of the USG to provide an orderly and continuing means of supplemental assistance to state and local governments in their responsibilities to alleviate the suffering and damage that result from major disasters or emergencies. It is the primary legal authority for federal participation in domestic disaster relief. Under the Stafford Act, the President may direct federal agencies, including DOD, to support disaster relief. DOD may be directed to provide assistance in one of three different scenarios: a Presidential declaration of a major disaster, a Presidential order to perform emergency work for the preservation of life and property, or a Presidential declaration of emergency. To obtain common-user airlift, non-DOD agencies submit requests IAW *Defense Transportation Regulation (DTR) 4500.9-R.*

4. Airland Delivery

a. **Airland is the preferred method of aerial delivery.** Planners should view airland delivery as the primary means for most air movements. In the airland delivery method, airlifted personnel and materiel are disembarked, unloaded, or unslung from an aircraft after it has landed or, in the case of vertical takeoff and landing aircraft, after it has entered a hover.

b. Airland delivery is usually the most efficient delivery method for moving equipment, personnel, and supplies for the following reasons:

(1) It allows a greater degree of unit integrity and the capability to rapidly employ units after landing.

(2) It carries the least risk of injuring personnel and damaging loads.

(3) It requires minimal specialized training and equipment for transported personnel.

(4) It seldom requires special rigging of materiel.

(5) It permits the maximum utilization of ACL by eliminating the volume and weight penalties of preparing loads for airdrop deliveries.

(6) It maximizes the opportunity to backhaul or evacuate cargo, patients, and personnel.

c. The principal disadvantages of air land operations are:

(1) It requires airfields or LZs that are moderately level or unobstructed and adequate for the anticipated operation.

(2) It may increase mission intervals, and thus the total time for delivery of a given force, depending on airfield size, offload equipment availability, and airfield support capability.

(3) It normally requires airlift mission support such as ground-handling and transportation assets.

(4) It prolongs exposure of aircraft, crews, and ground support personnel to air or ground attacks.

(5) It reduces available airlift flexibility when using uncontaminated aircraft to land in a contaminated environment. Once an aircraft is contaminated it will not be allowed to be operated in an uncontaminated environment.

(6) It may require additional sorties to deliver MHE.

d. When planning air land operations, consideration should be given, but not limited, to the following:

(1) The duration and location of the operation.

(2) The type and amount of cargo or number of passengers for delivery.

(3) The number and type airlift assets available and aircrews and ground crews available to fly and service them.

(4) The desired phasing of forces into the operating area.

(5) The expected threats throughout the mission.

(6) Force protection requirements.

(7) APOE/en route/APOD airfield capabilities to include:

(a) Working MOG reflecting the number of aircraft that can cycle through an airfield in a given time based on services available.

(b) Available MHE.

(c) POL storage and dispensing capability.

(d) Available transportation assets to transport cargo and personnel.

(e) Pavement strength and obstacle clearance requirements.

(f) Aircraft servicing, maintenance, and damage repair capabilities.

(g) Crew rest facilities.

(8) Airspace considerations, to include the ability to control airspace in the absence of ATC facilities.

For further information on TTP for terminal airfield ATC, see FM 3-52.3/MCRP 3-25A/NTTP 3-56.3/AFTTP 3-2.23, Multi-Service Tactics, Techniques, and Procedures for Joint Air Traffic Control.

(9) The weather conditions.

(10) Night operation/night vision device requirements.

(11) Aircrew survival measures, including escape and evasion points, routes, corridors, and safe haven locations.

e. Air land operations generally fall within the following four concepts:

(1) **Hub and Spoke Operations.** Intertheater air land operations normally offload personnel and materiel at a main operating location within the theater. Subsequently, intratheater airlift moves designated personnel and equipment to forward operating locations, an employment concept referred to as a **hub and spoke** operation (see Figure IV-1). Hub and spoke operations allow planners to maximize the capabilities of each aircraft type and they provide a safe location for transloading operations by avoiding flights into high-threat or contaminated locations. This is particularly important for nonmilitary aircraft which typically lack defensive countermeasure equipment.

(a) Hub and spoke operations permit flexible dispersion (to include last minute changes in requirements) between the various forward operating bases (FOBs).

(b) Units should consider the required MHE and transportation assets needed to transfer personnel, equipment, and cargo from one aircraft to another.

(2) **Direct Delivery.** Direct delivery involves airlifting personnel and materiel from ports of embarkation to forward-operating locations in the theater. By bypassing intermediary operating bases and the transshipment of payloads typically associated with hub and spoke operations (see Figure IV-1), direct delivery typically shortens in-transit time and reduces congestion at main operating bases. Direct delivery can use airland or airdrop delivery methods. For example, personnel can be airlifted from CONUS and delivered directly to the theater by airlanding or airdropping them at a forward operating location.

(a) Direct delivery is often the quickest method for delivery of TS cargo. While these operations are more complex, they can significantly reduce the GAMSS footprint by eliminating transshipping operations, reducing the number of diplomatic clearances required and, in most cases, decreasing closure time. Direct delivery is not, however, the best solution for large movements or when there are multiple FOBs that must be serviced.

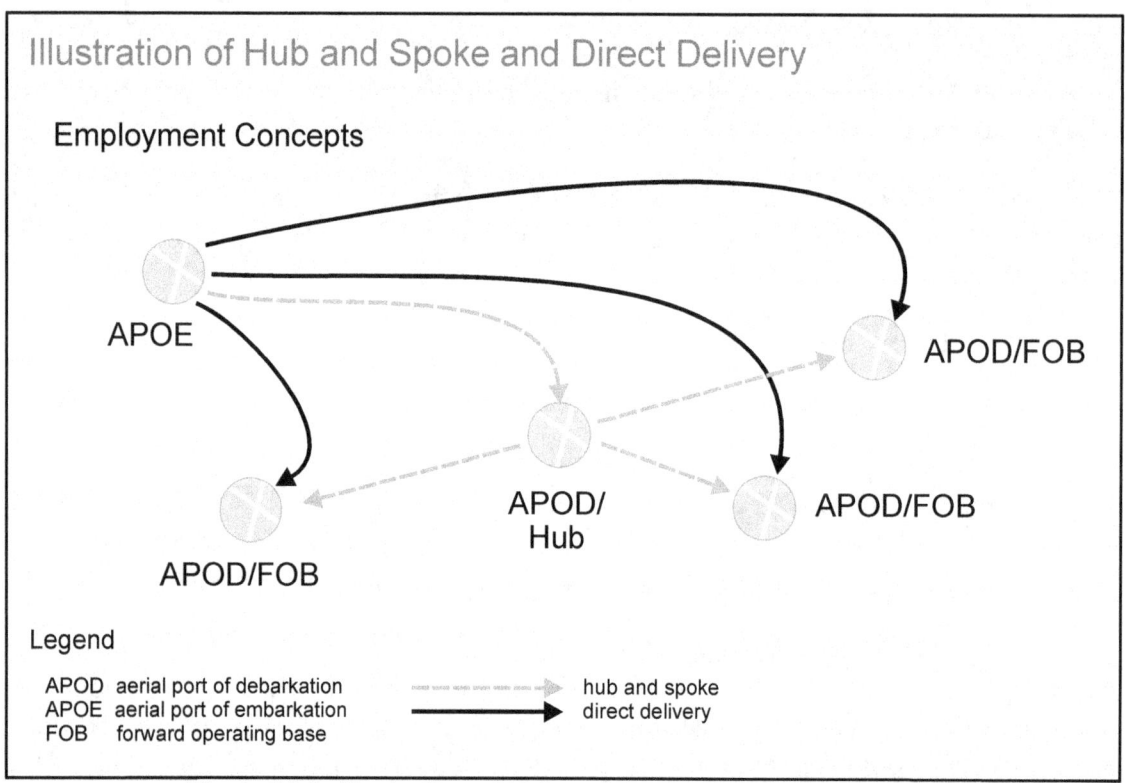

Figure IV-1. Illustration of Hub and Spoke and Direct Delivery

(b) Most direct delivery operations will require an air bridge and associated AR support. AR support will increase the number of aircraft required to accomplish the mission.

(3) **Stage Operations.** Aircraft ranges, crew requirements, and mission limitations may dictate the need for intermediate stops. This practice is also called lily pad operations (see Figure IV-2). The final leg into the AOR or JOA may terminate at the final destination or at a theater hub. These operations require en route support locations and may place a heavier burden on GAMSS.

(4) **Air Bridge.** Air bridge operations refer to flights between CONUS and OCONUS terminals where the receiver aircraft's range is augmented by an in-flight refueling on designated AR tracks (see Figure IV-3).

f. Planners should also consider the following for air land operations:

(1) Airfield and aerial port capabilities may result in mission delays and backlog cargo at intermediate or theater offload terminals.

(2) AR and airlift forces have finite maintenance and regeneration cycles, which may quickly be exceeded.

(3) GAMSS forces have limited organic resources and can only operate "barebase" terminals for limited time periods.

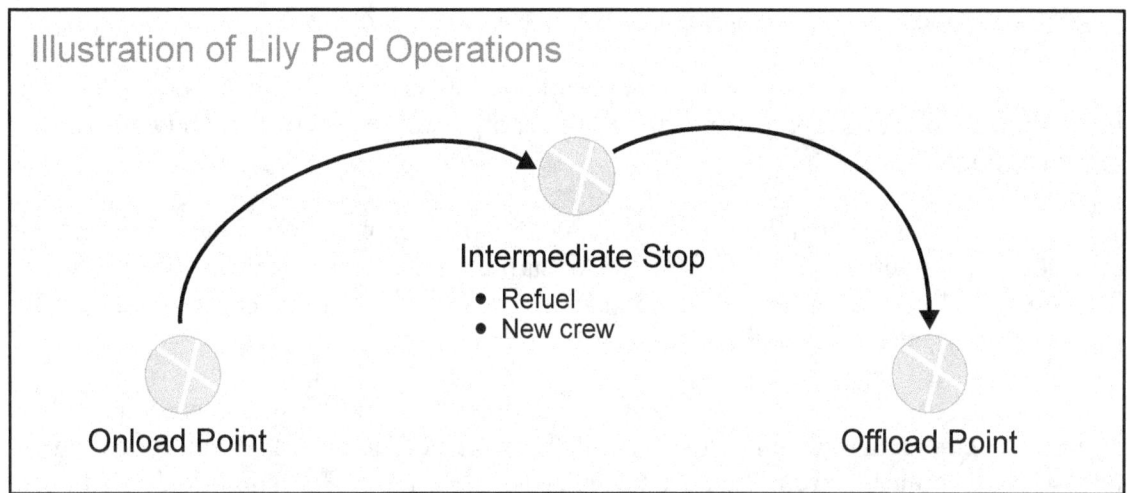

Figure IV-2. Illustration of Lily Pad Operations

g. For movement planning purposes, airlift aircraft load planning considerations are either administrative-loading or combat-loading.

(1) Administrative-loading gives primary consideration to using airlift assets most efficiently. Administrative-loading maximizes use of volumes and weight capacities of airlift aircraft and their ACL without regard to ground force tactical considerations. Routine air movement is usually unopposed and uses secure airfields or well established LZs; the majority of these missions involve the administrative loading of troops and equipment.

(2) Combat-loading arranges personnel and materiel to arrive at their intended destination in an order and condition so they are ready for immediate use. Combat-loading maximizes the combat readiness of the organizations and equipment being moved and stresses effectiveness. Airlift forces can move combat-loaded units to maximize their readiness for immediate combat operations. Given the assumption of immediate combat, user requirements should dictate scheduling and load planning.

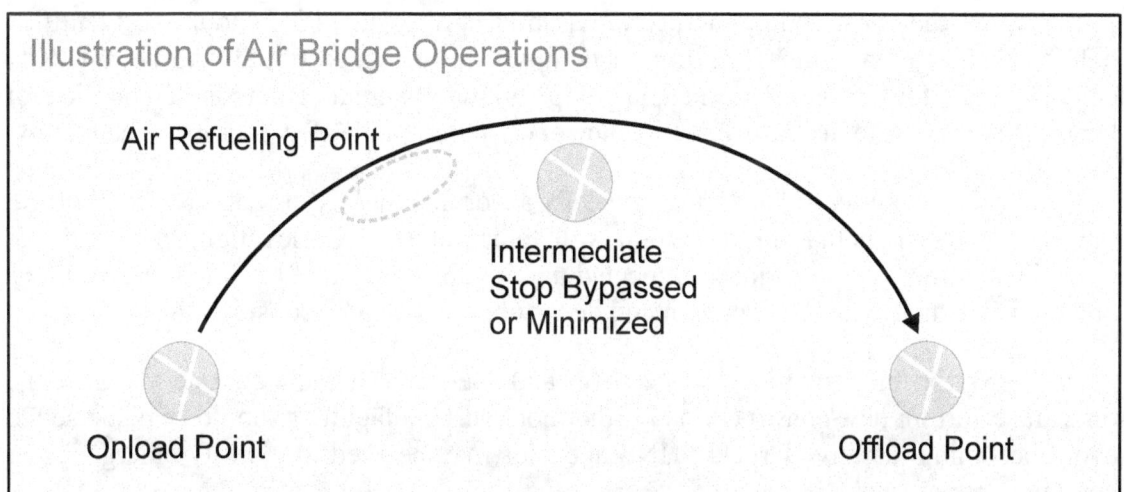

Figure IV-3. Illustration of Air Bridge Operations

h. The following are considerations when selecting a LZ:

(1) The JFC determines the most suitable LZ locations. The selected sites must meet aircraft operational requirements, ground component requirements, and construction considerations.

(a) If an airfield is to be constructed, the supported component engineer, the JFC-designated representative, and the USAF staff engineer must agree on its specific site. The supported component engineer controls the selected site until the designated airlift representative accepts use of the LZ.

(b) Aircraft may have to use LZ facilities before construction is completed. In addition to emergency landing situations, delivery of additional construction equipment, emergency supplies, or reinforcing units may be necessary. The supported component construction engineer and the designated airlift representative should jointly agree to such use.

(c) When established construction requirements have been met and the designated airlift representative accepts the LZ, control of the LZ passes to the airlift mission commander. The JFC staff assigns an appropriate engineer force to repair and maintain the critical landing surfaces, taxiway, and hardstands. The composition and size of the unit will depend on the threat situation, type and location of the LZ, availability of engineering forces, expected LZ use, and weather.

(2) Although the senior planning headquarters assigns the general landing area, subordinate units usually designate specific LZs. Desirable characteristics of LZs are ease of identification from the air; suitable airfield capabilities; a straight, unobstructed, and secure approach for aircraft; and close proximity to ground objectives. Depending upon mission requirements, some LZs may be developed into more sophisticated facilities.

For additional information, see JP 3-34, Joint Engineer Operations.

(3) LZs should be classified according to the applicable aircraft and airfield criteria furnished by the construction engineer. Essential airland facilities should be identified before the operation begins. Minimum facilities are provided initially to permit early occupancy and for safe and efficient landing operations. Plans and orders should provide for later improvements to increase the efficiency of operations and safety factors of the facility.

(4) Suitability of LZ dimensions vary according to the types of aircraft involved. Factors considered include aircraft ground roll, temperature, field elevation, and nature and conditions of the landing surface. Expected maximum takeoff and landing gross weights, obstructions, and terrain on approach and departure must also be considered.

(5) Existing facilities, such as roads and open areas, should be used to reduce the time and effort for new construction. Furthermore, airland facilities should be dispersed to avoid becoming lucrative targets. HNS agencies may be used to identify emergency or contingency runways.

5. Airdrop

In the various airdrop methods, airlifted personnel and materiel are deployed from aircraft still in flight.

a. Airdrop is often militarily advantageous.

(1) It permits sustainment deliveries to units operating away from airfields and LZs.

(2) It permits the delivery of combat forces and materiel, concentrated and in mass, in minimum space and time (often with the element of surprise).

(3) It may allow airlift aircraft to deploy personnel and materiel in conditions of poor visibility that would otherwise preclude air land operations.

(4) Medium/high altitude airdrop methods enable aircraft to remain above some low altitude threats.

(5) It permits critical cargo delivery by an uncontaminated aircraft into a contaminated LZ or airfield.

b. In relation to airland delivery, airdrop delivery has several disadvantages.

(1) It carries an increased risk of injury to personnel or damage to cargo.

(2) It requires special training for the riggers, transported personnel, and the aircrews.

(3) It can limit ACL utilization substantially because of the special rigging required for airdropped materiel.

(4) It requires more mission planning time due to the complexity of airdrop operations.

(5) If employed by a large formation, it represents an operational level risk. Detection and successful attack by the adversary could rob the theater campaign of two critical assets: the airlift force and the unit and/or materiel being carried. Accordingly, the decision to use the airdrop method is predicated on determining if a user's requirements justify the risk to, and expenditure of, scarce and costly airdrop resources.

(6) It is less precise than with airland delivery, and carries greater potential for unplanned dispersion.

c. **Responsibilities.** The JFC makes the decision to continue, cancel, or postpone airdrop operations based on the recommendations of the ground and air component commanders. The airborne force commander and airlift mission commander should coordinate with each other throughout the aerial delivery planning and mission execution on matters such as:

(1) Flight routing to/from the objective area to include re-attack options.

(2) DZ size and geographic relationship to the initial objective.

(3) Terrain conditions on the DZ that could cause an unacceptable number of injuries, excessive equipment damage or loss, or other deployment delays.

(4) Routes to the DZ, terrain obstructions, ease of zone identification, and adversary defenses.

(5) Earliest possible collaboration on intelligence matters, to include requirements for intelligence data, information, and geospatial products.

(6) Identification of MC cargo and a "go or no-go" decision point.

d. The airlift mission commander should also coordinate with the supported force commander before determining the tactics to employ. Many factors influence this decision, including the size of DZs, surrounding terrain features, tactical scheme of maneuver, enemy air defenses, and en route and objective area weather.

e. **C2.** Clear C2 authorities are essential. The airdrop system should be designed to be responsive in supporting requirements. Airdrop resupply is a joint action between the USAF component and the component being supported. Supported components are responsible for providing required supplies, rigging them for airdrop, and delivering them to the departure airfield. The supported component is also responsible for loading the supplies onto the airdrop aircraft under supervision of USAF personnel.

(1) Units requesting airdrop resupply have responsibilities to accomplish both before and after submission of airdrop requests. Before submitting requests, units should determine:

(a) Supplies and equipment needed;

(b) Location of DZ; and

(c) Time and date airdrop is desired.

(2) After airdrop requests are submitted, units:

(a) Prepare and secure the DZ;

(b) Control the DZ in the absence of a USAF STT. DZST personnel may operate DZs under visual meteorological conditions and instrument meteorological conditions (peacetime training based upon equipment availability) for single-ship aircraft and formations up to and including three aircraft);

(c) Recover airdropped supplies and equipment; and

(d) Recover, retrograde, or destroy airdrop equipment.

f. **Airdrop Methods.** Airdrop is an alternate to airland for delivering personnel, equipmen,t and supplies. The type of airdrop (low or medium-high altitude, low velocity, high velocity, free drop, single ship or multi-ship) depends on the threat, the required payload, the accuracy required, and whether mass is required on the DZ. Units requesting airdrop should request a capability. The supporting command should task the appropriate asset and tacticians should determine the appropriate method of airdrop.

(1) **Personnel Airdrop.** Personnel airdrops use static line or free fall procedures. In general, static line airdrops occur from fixed wing/rotary wing aircraft at altitudes below 1,500 feet above ground level (AGL) and are often used to minimize paratroopers' exposure to ground threats while under the canopy. Conversely, free fall airdrops normally occur above 5000 feet AGL. Specialized free fall procedures (high altitude low-opening/high-altitude high-opening) may be used to insert personnel as part of a clandestine operation.

For additional information, see applicable Service manuals and directives (i.e., FM 3-21.220, Static Line Parachuting Techniques and Training, *and ATTP 3-18.11,* Special Forces Military Free-Fall Operations).

(2) **Heavy Equipment Airdrop.** Heavy equipment loads consist of vehicles, equipment or supplies rigged for airdrop on Type V platforms which are extracted singularly or sequentially by extraction parachutes.

(3) **CDS Airdrop.** A CDS airdrop is a gravity assisted airdrop utilizing A-22 containers rigged to different parachutes. There are two basic rigging varieties for CDS: CDS (using low rate of fall chutes) and high-velocity container delivery system (HVCDS) in which the loads are cushioned with extra energy absorbing material and contain supplies that can withstand high velocity impact. A subset of the HVCDS is the low-cost aerial delivery system (LCADS) which uses one-time-use, low cost parachutes to deploy materiel.

(a) **Extracted Container Delivery System (XCDS).** XCDS airdrop deploys standard CDS bundles from the aircraft ramp and door at very low altitudes via a tow-plate initiated extraction. XCDS provides a circular error (CE) within 100 meters while enabling a higher density/smaller dispersal footprint on the DZ.

(b) **Low Cost, Low Altitude (LCLA).** LCLA airdrop is an aerial delivery system consisting of low-weight airdrop bundles deployed from the aircraft ramp and door at very low altitudes, enabling CE accuracy within 100 meters. This airdrop is appropriate for employment within or near a FOB or close to troops.

(4) **Improved Container Delivery System (ICDS) Airdrop.** An ICDS airdrop uses standard A-22 containers (up to 10,000 pounds in weight) rigged with various types of parachutes. The *"improved"* aspect is achieved by using joint precision airdrop system (JPADS) software to leverage Air Force Weather Agency wind data and dropsonde GPS telemetry data to calculate a more accurate ballistic wind and a more refined release point.

The resultant effect is potential increased drop accuracy from low and high altitude airdrops (chute-type dependent) operations, in day/night/instrument meteorological conditions/visual meteorological conditions. Similar to conventional CDS, ICDS may be rigged as CDS or HVCDS, or LCADS. LCADS offers the accuracy and threat mitigation benefits of ICDS while also mitigating the equipment retrograde requirement through the use of one-time use chutes.

(5) **JPADS.** JPADS is a family of GPS-guided, self-maneuvering systems. The overall basic system consists of a common mission planner, an airborne guidance unit, and multiple steerable parachute/parafoil systems. Certain systems require dropsonde employment. Flight profiles can vary significantly with system type utilized. Airspace deconfliction is a critical JPADS employment operations planning factor. While JPADS is not a universal airdrop solution, it is the preferred method for high altitude drops over difficult terrain where limiting the exposure of ground troops to enemy fire and minimizing risk to aircraft and aircrews are at a premium.

(6) **Free Fall Airdrop.** Free fall airdrop involves dropping small items such as packaged meals or unbreakable objects like hay bales without the use of a parachute.

(a) **Leaflet Airdrop.** Leaflets are used in support of military support IOs. The required leaflet dispersion pattern is based on leaflet size, paper weight utilized, target/coverage area size, and wind speed. These factors impact drop altitude and possible run-in headings. An accurate weather forecast is the single most important requirement.

(b) **Tri-wall Aerial Distribution System (TRIADS) Airdrop.** TRIADS is used to airdrop containers of humanitarian daily rations during humanitarian airdrop operations. It uses standard CDS procedures with boxes rigged to destruct at the end of a static line as they exit the aircraft, causing their contents to be dispersed into the air. Like leaflet drops, target/coverage area size is a factor when determining drop altitude.

g. **DZ.** A DZ is a specified area used for the aerial delivery of personnel, equipment, or supplies through the use of airdrop. DZ size and selection are the shared responsibility of the supporting and supported JFCs and depend on the load being dropped, method of delivery, dispersal pattern, and the level of risk the JFC is willing to accept. A physical survey, accomplished by a qualified surveyor, and a safety-of-flight review are required before a DZ can be approved for use. The supported force is responsible for DZ establishment, operation, safety, and elimination or acceptance of ground hazards associated with the DZ. The airlift mission commander is responsible for the safety-of-flight review.

(1) **DZ Types.** There are several different types of DZs that can be tailored to specific operations and locations.

(a) **Rectangular.** DZs are normally rectangular due to the longer length requirements. These DZs have one axis of flight that permit run-ins from opposite directions.

Container delivery system bundles departing a C-17 during an airdrop mission.

(b) **Area.** An area DZ, illustrated in Figure IV-4, consists of a start point (point A), an end point (point B), and a prearranged flight path (line of flight) over a series of acceptable drop sites between these points. The distance between points A and B generally should not exceed 15 nautical miles or 28 kilometers, and changes in ground elevation along the line of flight should not exceed 300 feet or 90 meters. The user may want the drop to occur at any location between point A and point B within ½ nautical mile of centerline. Aircrew use pre-briefed signals to identify the drop location.

(c) **Circular.** A circular DZ, shown in Figure IV-5, has multiple run-in headings and is inherently random. Mission requirements and usable terrain govern its size. The radius of a circular DZ corresponds to the minimum required distance from the point of impact (PI) to one of the trailing edge corners of a rectangular DZ for the same type and number of loads being dropped. In other words, the entire DZ box fits inside the circle. Water DZs are normally circular in shape. The PI of a circular DZ is normally at the DZ center.

(d) **Random Approach.** Random approach DZs are circular, square, or rectangular and large enough to permit multiple run-in headings. Any axis of approach may be used as long as the resulting DZ meets minimum criteria for the load being airdropped. The PI is normally placed at the DZ center point.

(e) **JPADS.** JPADS (guided systems) DZs are typically circular. The PI is located at the center point. Some JPADS multi-platform loads/capabilities may drive

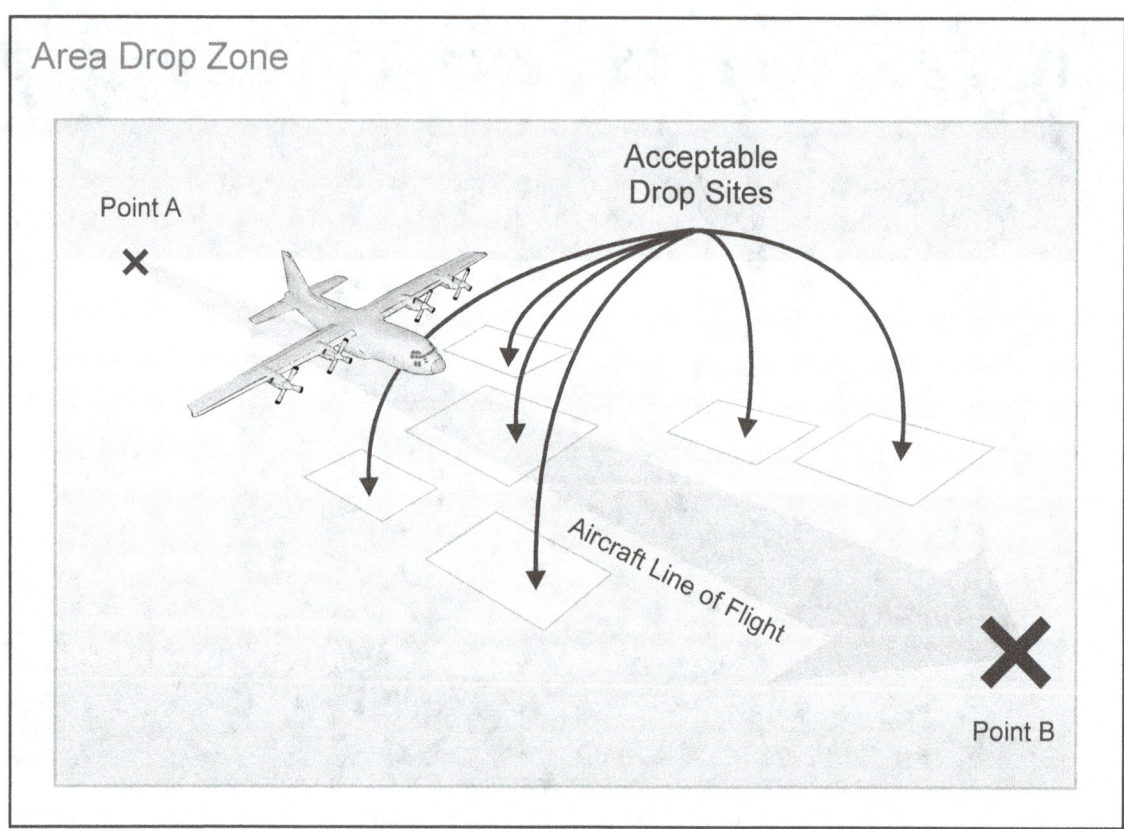

Figure IV-4. Area Drop Zone

elliptical DZs, approximated by rectangular surveyed boundaries. For JPADS/improvised CDS airdrops, an airdrop damage estimate (ADE) is required. This is necessary to mitigate the risk to people, buildings, and equipment near or on the DZ if a chute or guidance unit fails. It is critical that the ADE be coordinated between the supporting and supported force commander.

(f) **Tactical.** Tactical DZs are used during exercises and contingencies to support highly mobile ground forces. These DZs are evaluated and approved for use in an abbreviated manner, but they still require a physical survey and safety-of-flight review. Tactical DZs may be created within the boundaries of an existing surveyed DZ if needed to accomplish a particular mission. In this case, only a safety-of-flight review is required. Tactical DZs will not be used for routine training.

(g) **Special Purpose.** Special purpose DZs include: water, military free-fall, open field, tree jump, and mission DZs. These are used by specially qualified personnel for training to duplicate conditions that could be encountered during operational missions.

(2) **Airdrop Considerations.** A wide variety of factors determine the conduct of airdrop operations.

(a) **Drop Airspeeds.** Specific airdrop airspeeds for each type aircraft are published in appropriate Service manuals or technical orders. Except in emergencies, aircraft should not deviate from these established airspeeds. Deceleration to prescribed drop

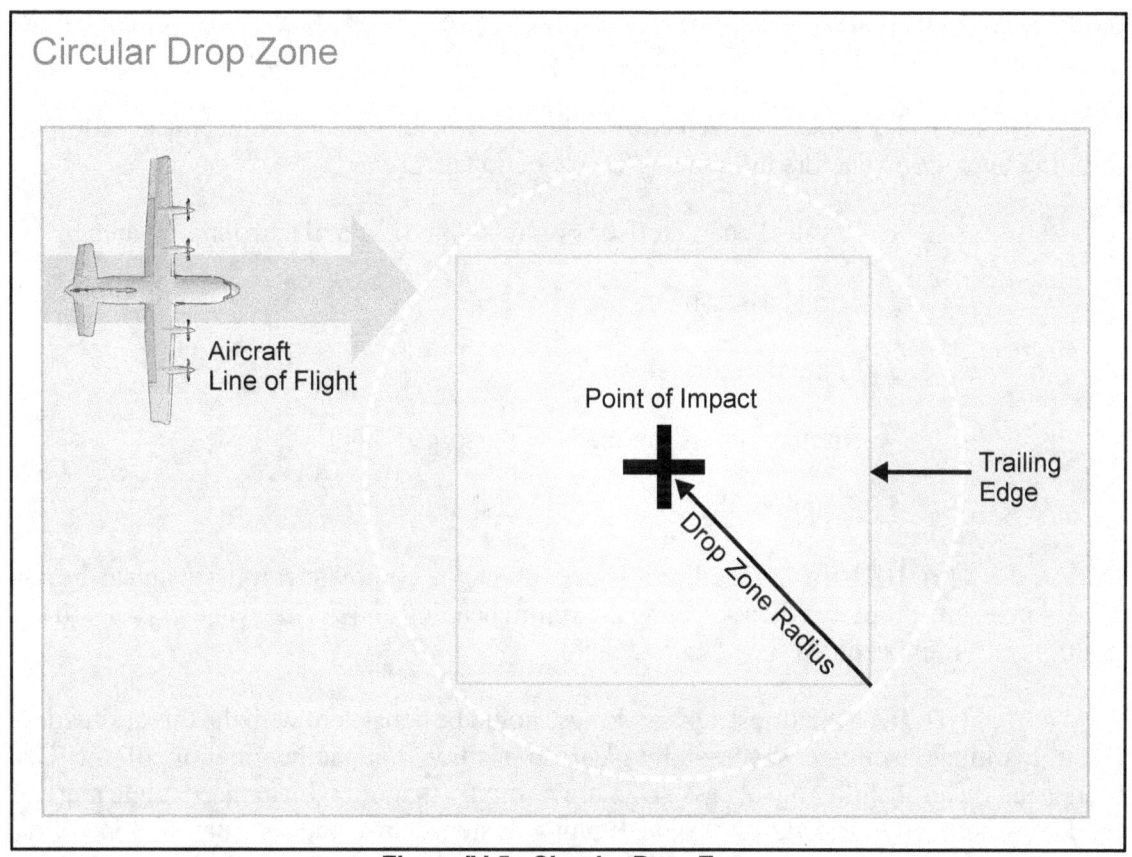

Figure IV-5. Circular Drop Zone

airspeed and attainment of level flight altitude are required to provide a stable platform for the actual airdrop of personnel, supplies, or equipment.

(b) **DZ Wind. DZ wind information is critical to airdrop accuracy** and aircrews must consider wind data from all available sources when determining the computed air release point. In addition to inflight wind data, aircrews are normally provided with DZ wind information from ground sources (such as STTs or DZSTs) which includes surface winds and the computed mean effective winds. Additionally, ground sources can relay indications of possible wind shears or local phenomena that could affect wind direction or speed and, ultimately, impact upon airdrop or mission success. Airdrop operations may not be feasible during conditions of strong or gusty surface winds. The JFC, based on recommendations by the ground and air component commanders, may accept the high risk, cancel, or postpone the operation because of excessive wind velocity on the DZ.

(c) **Drop Altitudes. The airborne force commander and airlift mission commander establish minimum altitudes for airdropping personnel and materiel IAW established criteria.** Minimum altitudes for airdrop operations are based on the operational requirements of the personnel and cargo airdrop systems used. In a high-risk, high-threat environment, survivability of airlift aircraft may require dropping parachutists and equipment at the lowest possible altitude. However, if the threat situation permits, aircraft performing normal low-altitude, low-velocity airdrop operations should drop above the minimum altitude to increase load survivability. Higher altitudes increase load time under canopy and allow more time for stabilization of parachute malfunctions.

(d) **DZ Size and Selection.** The JFC determines the general area for the airborne operation. Factors influencing DZ selection are:

1. Physical characteristics of available DZs and surrounding areas;

2. Threat assessment;

3. Method of air delivery;

4. Number of airdrop loads or personnel; and

5. Length of the desirable dispersion pattern.

(e) **DZ Run-in Heading.** The ground force commander must evaluate the risk to personnel and property when selecting the run-in heading and decide whether or not to use multiple run-in procedures (i.e., "racetracks").

(f) **DZ Markings.** DZ markings should be consistent with the threat situation. Clear markings facilitate successful visual acquisition and authentication of the DZ, increasing the probability of success. DZs are normally marked with a raised angle marker, marker panels, omnidirectional visible lighting systems, or electronic navigational aids. Virtually any type of overt or covert lighting or visual marking system is acceptable if all participating units are briefed and concur in its use. Other day markings or visual acquisition devices include, but are not limited to, colored smoke, mirrors, or any reflective or contrasting marker panel, such as a space blanket. In some cases geographical points may be used. Night markings or acquisition aids may include a light gun, flares, fire or fire pots, railroad fuses, flashlights, and chemical lights. STTs or drop zone controllers (DZCs) may also use specialized clandestine infrared lighting systems. Electronic markings may be used for either day or night operations. A verbally initiated release system may be used with no markings. Airlift crews may be called upon to conduct airdrop operations on an unmarked, blind DZ.

h. **DZ Communications.** In general, airdrop missions are flown as planned with minimum non-secure radio transmissions. Detailed mission planning, pre-briefed operating procedures, and use of formation station keeping equipment can eliminate many flight-following and into-formation transmissions. Radio contact with the drop aircraft should be limited to safety of flight requirements or issues affecting airborne force employment (e.g., ATC directions of mission changes). DZ winds or other information may be broadcasted in the blind at coordinated times prior to the drop.

i. **DZ C2.** The USAF DZC represents the appropriate commander as provided in the mission directive. The DZC observes and evaluates all factors that may adversely affect the safety of the operation and ensures transmission of weather information when required. The DZC is normally a USAF combat controller or AMLO who is authorized to control all airdrops for any US or allied military force. AMLOs are qualified to perform DZC duties during joint and unilateral airdrop operations.

j. **DZ Sequencing and Separation of Personnel and Equipment.** Separation times between personnel and equipment and the sequence of the drop are important considerations in an airdrop mission. Terrain and threat assessment dictate whether personnel or equipment are airdropped first. Combination drops occur when parachutists exit from the cargo ramp immediately after release of equipment. Equipment and personnel can also be dropped from separate aircraft on the same DZ simultaneously if equipment loads are sufficiently separated to provide adequate clearance for personnel. However, such a COA requires the concurrence of the supporting and supported commanders.

6. **Planning Considerations for Airborne Assaults and Follow-on Air Land Operations**

a. **Planning airlift operations is a complicated process involving a few basic principles and numerous interdependent considerations. Service components must facilitate their airlift movement process.** This responsibility includes performing and arranging to:

(1) Bring units and materiel to departure terminals;

(2) Prepare those resources for air movement;

(3) Provide support services (meals, medical, billeting, and other appropriate services) to transient and arriving units;

(4) Receive and transport units and materiel from arrival terminals; and

(5) Prepare all manifests, movement documents, and reports related to the actual movement.

b. The purpose of these actions is to move component resources expeditiously, with minimum expenditure of resources and minimum exposure to hostile actions. **Responsibility for controlling movements does not equate to command authority over airlift forces.** Studies, concepts, and OPLANs for employment of forces are prepared to cover possible missions and locations. Detailed planning for specific operations is performed by the participating component commands and subordinate commands; to enhance efficiency, all participants should make maximum use of existing plans.

c. **Consider these principles when planning for airlift movements:**

(1) Minimize movement congestion and vulnerability by reducing the time units and materiel spend en masse at forward terminals and synchronize the positioning of units and material with airlift capability.

(2) Maximize the productivity and survivability of the airlift fleet by minimizing aircraft ground times at forward locations.

(3) Minimize sortie requirements by repackaging all materiel for air shipment; ensuring combat personnel travel with their maximum authorized individual loads of rations, ammunition, or other personal protective equipment; and splitting units into air-essential and surface movement echelons (whenever possible).

(4) Ensure personnel are adequately fed, rested, and protected at en route stops.

(5) Deploy personnel and communications equipment necessary to track and report on all air movements.

d. Different missions will require the use of different airlift assets. The Services possess a variety of fixed- and rotary-wing platforms capable of performing the air mobility role.

(1) The main advantage of fixed-wing aircraft over ground surface transportation modes is that they combine speed (250 to 500 knots, depending on aircraft type) and the ability to carry substantial to very large cargo capacities (7 to over 100 tons, also depending on aircraft type). This provides the capability to quickly move large amounts of personnel and materiel over greater distances. Airlift can also be employed to reduce the need for ground convoy operations that are vulnerable to enemy attack. The combination of their speed and tactics also enhances their survivability, while their range generally allows them to be based in relatively secure and logistically easier-to-support rear areas. The main disadvantages are their terminal requirements, which can limit their flexibility, and their size and limited maneuverability, which increases their vulnerability to ground and air attack. These disadvantages are particularly pronounced for the larger transports. Under most circumstances smaller transports, such as the C-130, are usually suited to a sustained intratheater airlift role, and the larger transports are best suited for the intertheater airlift role.

(2) In a CBRN contaminated environment, plan to avoid contaminating air mobility aircraft, thus preserving limited assets for future use. Avoid air land operations into contaminated airfields by airdropping critical supplies and equipment or shifting deliveries to uncontaminated airfields (consider use of austere LZs such as highway landing strips and dirt and/or gravel LZ construction).

(3) The Services and United States Special Operations Command also operate rotary-wing and tiltrotor aircraft, such as the UH-1, H-60, V-22, CV-22, CH-46, CH-47, and CH-53, which possess intrinsic intratheater airlift capabilities. Rotary-wing and tiltrotor aircraft can be useful for intratheater purposes for the following reasons:

(a) Their ability to operate at smaller undeveloped LZs increases their flexibility and often reduces ground-transit times for their loads;

(b) Their ability to transport personnel and materiel to and from forward-deployed ships increases expeditionary flexibility;

(c) Their terrain-hugging flight capabilities enhance their survivability in certain threat situations; and

(d) Their ability to sling-load some types of materiel allows them to pick up and deliver loads with minimal ground-handling delays.

(4) However, in relation to fixed-wing aircraft, the inherent aerodynamic inefficiencies of rotary-wing aircraft sharply restrict payload and range capabilities. In addition, their mechanical characteristics give them a high ratio of support-man-hours to flight-hours. Consequently, rotary-winged assets:

(a) Usually are not suited to sustained airlift operations beyond about 50-100 nautical miles from a refueling point;

(b) Usually require more maintenance hours per hour of flight time; and

(c) Are usually based at LZs not well suited to large-scale, sustained fixed-wing airlift operations.

(5) For these reasons, airlift-capable rotary-wing and tilt rotor assets are normally assigned as organic combat and combat support elements to surface combat organizations. Thus, in deciding to use the capabilities of any organic rotary-wing assets to support the intratheater airlift effort, the JFC should consider their vital importance to their assigned organizations, as well as their utility to specific airlift missions. Intratheater airlift requirements that might best be filled by rotary-wing aircraft could include large requirement, short-distance operations, such as resupplying ships at sea and unloading ships at undeveloped water terminals, or routine small-payload operations to sites not collocated with LZs, such as daily courier flights to deployed air defense units.

Additional information on air assault operations can be found in JP 3-18, Joint Forcible Entry Operations.

Intentionally Blank

CHAPTER V
AIR REFUELING

> *"I had to fly nine sorties on the day the St. Mihiel offensive started…We all wished we could refuel somehow without having to return to our bases just when the action got interesting."*
>
> **Lieutenant John Richter, US Army Air Service Pilot in WWI**

1. General

a. AR allows air assets to rapidly reach any trouble spot around the world with less dependence on forward staging bases. Furthermore, AR significantly expands the force options available to a commander by increasing the range, payload, loiter time, and flexibility of other aircraft.

b. Because AR increases the range of other aircraft, many types of aircraft may be based at locations well outside the range of an adversary threat. AR allows some aircraft to participate in contingency operations without having to forward-deploy. Operations based from CONUS or established main operating bases reduce the theater logistics requirements, thereby simplifying sustainment efforts. Positioning forces outside the adversary's reach permits a greater portion of combat assets to concentrate on offensive rather than defensive action. As a result of the reduced need to forward-deploy forces, AR reduces force protection requirements as well.

c. Although other Services and nations maintain some organic AR capability, the USAF possesses the overwhelming preponderance of common-user AR assets. With boom and drogue capability, these assets are capable of refueling most USAF, Navy, and Marine Corps aircraft, and can accommodate most foreign aircraft.

d. **All USAF tanker aircraft are capable of performing an airlift role to augment core airlift assets.** Under the dual-role concept, AR aircraft can transport a combination of passengers and cargo while performing AR. In some circumstances, it may be more efficient to employ AR aircraft strictly in an airlift role. Deploying AR units may be tasked to use their organic capacity to transport unit personnel and support equipment or passengers and cargo from other units. AR aircraft may also be used to support USTRANSCOM airlift requirements such as routine channel operations or SAAMs.

e. AR permits aircraft to operate beyond their unrefueled ranges and permits larger takeoff payloads and added endurance. By enabling their payload to be maximized, the combat potential of receiver aircraft is significantly increased.

f. Force extension is the AR of one tanker by another and is the most efficient means to provide deployment support, given a limited number of tanker aircraft. This capability can be used whenever the fuel requirements of the escorting tanker and its receivers exceed the tanker's takeoff fuel capacity. Since takeoff fuel is limited by the amount of payload carried, dual-role tankers may require force extension. Not all tankers are refuelable. All KC-10s are refuelable and a small number of KC-135s are equipped as receivers and therefore can be force extended. Whenever possible, force extension missions should be planned along air bridge routes to use tankers supporting air bridge movements.

g. **Components of the AR Force. The majority of the USAF's AR assets are assigned to USAF Reserve and ANG units.**

(1) **Active Duty Forces.** Similar to airlift forces, CDRUSTRANSCOM has COCOM of most CONUS-based active duty AR forces and delegates OPCON to AMC/CC who further delegates OPCON to 18 AF/CC (AFTRANS). Similarly, theater-assigned AR forces come under COCOM of their GCC (e.g., Commander, USEUCOM or Commander, USPACOM) and under OPCON of the theater COMAFFOR (e.g., USAFs in Europe or Pacific numbered air forces). These forces perform core and specialized AR missions and are readily available for tasking and deployment. In addition to the USAF, the Navy, and Marine Corps possess some organic AR resources, which may also augment joint AR operations.

(2) **Air Force Reserve and ANG Forces.** During crises, volunteers or activated AFRC and/or ANG units augment the active duty AR force, providing substantial increases in AR capacity. AFRC and ANG personnel train to the same standards as the active duty AR force. Peacetime access to AFRC and ANG forces is provided through a system of volunteerism or mobilization authorization for non-wartime events such as domestic emergencies and preplanned missions. Major contingencies, however, normally require activation of AFRC and/or ANG units.

2. Air Refueling Operations

AR's contribution to air power is based on the force enabling and force multiplying effects of increased range, payload, and endurance provided to refueled aircraft. **AR forces conduct both intertheater and intratheater AR operations.**

a. **Intertheater AR.** Intertheater AR supports the long-range movement of combat and combat support aircraft between theaters, or between theaters and JOAs. Intertheater AR operations also support global strike missions and airlift assets in an air bridge. AR enables deploying aircraft to fly nonstop to their destination, reducing closure time.

b. **Intratheater AR.** Intratheater AR supports operations within a GCC's AOR by extending the range, payload, and endurance of combat and combat support assets. Both theater-assigned and USTRANSCOM-assigned AR aircraft can perform these operations. When USTRANSCOM-assigned AR forces participate in these operations, they are typically attached to the GCC who exercises OPCON over these forces through the COMAFFOR. Although the primary purpose is to refuel combat air forces operating within the theater, consideration should be given to the best utilization of the tanker fleet to meet the President's and SecDef's objectives.

c. **Anchor Areas and AR Tracks.** AR is normally conducted in one of two ways: in an anchor area or along an AR track. While AR is normally conducted in friendly airspace,

Air refueling missions in United States Central Command's area of responsibility refuel almost 74,000 aircraft per year.

missions may require operations over hostile territory and in contested airspace. Anchor areas and tracks may place tankers in an extremely vulnerable position and should be limited to friendly airspace when possible. AR missions over hostile territory should be conducted only after careful risk considerations and when at least regional air superiority is achieved.

(1) In anchor areas, the tanker flies a racetrack pattern within defined airspace while waiting for receiver aircraft to arrive. Once joined with the receiver, the tanker then flies in an expanded racetrack pattern while refueling the receiver. **Anchor AR is normally used for intratheater operations where airspace is confined or where receivers operate in a central location.** Anchor areas are best suited for small, highly maneuverable aircraft, especially in marginal weather conditions.

(2) An AR track is a published track or precoordinated series of navigation points, which can be located anywhere throughout the world. To maximize effectiveness, AR tracks will normally be placed along the receiver's route of flight. However, AR track location(s) must be balanced with tanker availability and basing to develop an integrated AR plan making the best use of limited receiver and tanker assets overall. AR along an AR track is the preferred method for intertheater operations.

(3) The tanker RV can be accomplished in multiple ways. For more information about RV procedures, see Allied Tactical Publication (ATP)-56, *Air to Air Refueling*.

d. **Tanker Formation Refueling.** Many missions require tankers to refuel their receivers while in a multiple-ship formation. Mission requirements may dictate several different types of tankers (boom and/or drogue equipped) and multiple receiver types (from a variety of nations) in the same formation. Formation refueling is one of the most demanding operations due to the number of aircraft in a confined block of airspace and because receiver aircraft may be constantly joining and leaving the formation. It also brings in additional planning factors and requires a significant amount of coordination to ensure smooth, safe execution of the mission.

e. **Joint and Multinational Operations.** Joint and multinational operations require teamwork, unity of effort, and principles that are fundamental to AR. When working with other Services and nations, there is a potential for differences in capabilities, procedures, and terminology, which may cause misunderstandings and confusion. Such operations therefore require a standard set of tactics, terminology, and procedures.

(1) For example, ATP-56, *Air to Air Refueling*, standardizes operating procedures and enhances interoperability among North Atlantic Treaty Organization member nations possessing AR assets. While the detailed procedures will depend on aircraft type, mode of employment, and national requirements, many allies should be able to achieve sufficient commonality so that a combined set of procedures can be developed. Commanders of a multinational force should agree as soon as possible on a common set of doctrine, tactics, and procedures for particular operations.

(2) In addition, airspace may be a primary limitation to AR operations. Standardizing multinational cell formation procedures allows a variety of AR assets to operate in compressed airspace. This is particularly important when large numbers of tankers may be refueling multiple receivers or formations of receivers. To generate the maximum combat airpower in multinational operations, all military capabilities must be integrated to the fullest extent. Multinational exercises are a key component to common doctrine and interoperability. These exercises should be used as often as feasible to foster a common understanding. The doctrine and procedures established by the multinational commander will provide additional flexibility, deployability, and sustainability in multinational air operations.

3. Air Refueling Missions

The Basic Missions of AR. AR is a critical force multiplier across the full range of global and theater employment scenarios. Tankers directly enhance the operational flexibility of US and allied/coalition strike, support, and surveillance aircraft. AR missions depicted in Figure V-1 represent the broad, fundamental, and continuing activities of the AR system. In the same manner, **the nearly unlimited flight endurance provided by tanker assets is an indispensable component of the US strategic airborne command post concept.** It provides the President and SecDef the ability to continue to direct military action from an airborne platform–regardless of the situation.

a. **Global Strike Support.** AR assets are a critical enabler for global strike operations (conventional or nuclear). For example, AR significantly increases the range and endurance of bomber aircraft, directly enhancing their flexibility to strike at distant targets and maximizing their operational utility for warfighter mission requirements. Tanker availability

Basic Air Refueling Missions

- Global strike support
- Air bridge support
- Aircraft deployment support
- Theater support to combat air forces
- Special operations support

Figure V-1. Basic Air Refueling Missions

can also be critical to overall mission success through support of a wide variety of support package aircraft refueling requirements. In addition, AR can mitigate operational risk for strike or support aircraft by decreasing reliance on OCONUS/forward basing locations. AR is key to US ability to rapidly strike targets in distant locations and recover to safe areas. The ability to perform long-range strike missions from CONUS is particularly crucial.

b. **Air Bridge Support.** An air bridge creates an ALOC linking CONUS and a theater, or any two theaters. AR makes possible accelerated air bridge operations since en route refueling stops for receivers are reduced or eliminated. It reduces reliance on forward staging bases, minimizes potential en route maintenance delays, and enables airlift assets to maximize their payloads. This significantly increases the efficiency of airlift operations by making possible the direct delivery of personnel and materiel.

c. **Aircraft Deployment Support.** AR assets can extend the range of deploying combat and combat support aircraft, allowing them to fly nonstop to an AOR or JOA. This capability increases the deterrent effect of CONUS-based forces and allows a rapid response to regional crises. The capability of air assets to fly nonstop to a theater may eliminate the need to obtain landing or overflight rights from foreign countries that may want to remain neutral in a given conflict. Successful execution of the USAF's aerospace expeditionary force concept, for example, is heavily dependent on the capabilities rendered through deployment support. Peacetime deployments of forces in support of rotations, exercises, or aircraft movements for logistic purposes are called Coronets. Coronets normally have long lead times for planning, tasking, and execution. Planners should use this time to maximize the overall efficiency of the movement for both receivers and tankers, while remembering their purpose is safe and effective movement of the receivers.

d. **Theater Support to Combat Air Forces.** Intratheater AR enables fighter aircraft to increase their range, endurance, and flexibility. During a combat operation, the highest priority for intratheater AR forces is normally supporting combat and combat support aircraft executing air operations. This is especially true during the initial phases of a conflict. Theater-based AR assets bolster the security of combat and combat support air assets by allowing them to be based beyond the range of adversary threats. Extending endurance reduces the number of sorties required, decreases ground support requirements at forward locations, and may reduce the number of aircraft deployed to an AOR.

(1) AR allows combat aircraft to carry a larger payload on initial takeoff by decreasing the amount of fuel carried in its tanks. Fuel necessary for mission range requirements is onloaded after takeoff on either pre-strike or post-strike refuelings. The ability to increase an aircraft's weapons load multiplies the combat force and combat efficiency of that aircraft.

(2) Operations ALLIED FORCE, OEF, and OIF have highlighted the importance of airspace required for AR, especially during combat support missions. A lack of AR airspace can limit the amount of combat and combat support sorties the JFACC is able to schedule and execute. Airspace planning for these operations includes sufficient allowances for ingress/egress of both receivers and tankers and allow deconflicting aircraft operating at significantly different speeds. Experience in OEF and OIF shows that without sufficient airspace deconfliction, the greatest threat to friendly forces can be from mid-air collisions with our own forces.

(3) Tankers allocated for theater support may be called upon to provide AR support to air bridge operations. The DIRMOBFOR must judge the capabilities of, and requirements for, tankers assigned or attached to the theater to determine their ability to provide air bridge support. When air bridge support operations will adversely impact theater support operations, the COMAFFOR must consider the JFC's overall operation or campaign objectives (such as defeating an adversary force or compelling an adversary to surrender), not just operational objectives (such as air superiority or shutting down the adversary's C2 system) when deciding how to allocate tanker missions.

e. **Special Operations Support.** AR enables SOF to maintain a long-range operating capability. The USAF maintains AR crews who are trained to air refuel fixed- and rotary-wing special operations aircraft. Successful mission completion requires special equipment, specialized crew training, and modified operational procedures.

f. **Other Associated AR Missions.** Additional taskings for AR aircraft include: emergency AR; airlift; AE; and combat search and rescue (CSAR).

(1) **Emergency AR.** Some AR aircraft may be kept on ground or airborne alert to provide short-notice support for airborne fuel emergencies. Fuel emergencies can result from missed refuelings, en route winds greater than planned, battle damage, or excessive time engaged with adversary aircraft or targets. While dedicated ground alert aircraft sometimes meet emergency AR requirements, excess fuel capacity of airborne tankers is another method of providing emergency AR capability. Putting more fuel in a tanker than is required to complete the mission, known as "tankering fuel," gives that aircraft an automatic, though limited, emergency refueling capability.

(a) **Intertheater Operations. OPCON of** intertheater AR will typically be delegated to 18 AF/CC (AFTRANS) with C2 provided by the 618 AOC (TACC). Whenever possible, intertheater missions should be planned either over, or in close proximity to, existing air bridge routes. This allows tankers positioned for air bridge support to also provide emergency AR support. When intertheater missions cannot be planned along air bridge routes and the mission is deemed important enough to provide emergency AR support, planners should use a combination of ground and airborne spare aircraft. Ground spare aircraft are maintained in various stages of readiness depending on mission requirements. Airborne spare aircraft consist of one or more tankers that accompany the AR formation, but do not participate in any ARs unless required to do so. No matter which option is used, the concepts must be adequately delineated in mission directives so tankers, receivers, and participating C2 elements are thoroughly familiar with procedures to be used in a fuel emergency.

(b) **Intratheater Operations.** The dynamic environment and quick tempo of intratheater operations provide a greater need for emergency AR support. The shorter distances involved and the larger number of available assets makes providing emergency AR support much easier to accomplish. The preferred method of providing emergency support is through a combination of ground and airborne aircraft.

<u>1.</u> Ground alert aircraft and crews primarily provide units with the capability to meet mission requirements when fuel emergencies occur due to battle damage or excessive time engaged with adversary aircraft or targets. The best tanker aircraft for ground alert duties are those capable of quick response times, high cruise speeds, and a takeoff fuel load large enough to accommodate all offloads. Ideally, ground spare aircraft should be capable of refueling drogue and boom type refueling on the same mission. Otherwise, units must maintain separate aircraft on ground alert, configured for each type of refueling. Ground alert tankers and crews can be dedicated solely to that function.

<u>2.</u> Refuelers are normally based well away from tactical operations areas for safety reasons. Ground spares might not be able to reach an area in a timely manner should tasked tankers not be able to provide adequate offload or receivers miss scheduled refuelings. Reliability tankers operate in a given area with no scheduled receivers and act as flying spares. Because of the cascading effects of the loss of AR, reliability tankers should be used when assets are available. If a reliability tanker can also accept fuel, the capability is leveraged through extended endurance.

(2) **Airlift.** Refueling platforms act as augmentation to the airlift fleet. This capability is most important during deployment operations when airlift requirements are highest and requirements for theater support refuelings are the lowest. During contingencies, commanders should continually evaluate tanker allocations to airlift missions, weighing the loss of assets from traditional tanker missions against the benefits gained by a larger, augmented airlift fleet. This evaluation must consider the objectives of the entire joint operation or campaign and not just those of the USAF component.

(a) Another key application of tanker aircraft in an airlift role occurs during tanker unit movements. Tanker units deploying to a theater or en route location will typically airlift their own support requirements under the integral tanker unit deployment concept. This allows tanker units to have key supplies and personnel on hand as soon as they arrive at their deployed location, and it relieves the air transportation system of at least a portion of their requirements.

(b) **Dual-Role Tanker.** Accomplishing airlift and AR on the same mission (dual-role operations) maximizes the full capabilities of tanker aircraft. Dual-role operations may be as simple as carrying opportune cargo or passengers on a routine intertheater AR mission, or it may be as complex as a fighter unit move. On Coronet missions, tankers carry a unit's personnel and equipment while escorting its fighters to a deployed location. Upon arrival, the tankers download their cargo and passengers who may immediately reconstitute and launch the deployed fighters. This allows arriving aircraft to be ready for follow-on missions quickly, simplifying required coordination for airlift support of deployments and reducing the number of dedicated airlift aircraft required to support an operation.

(3) **AE.** KC-135 and KC-10 tankers can be used for AE when crewed by a fully qualified and current AE crew using AE equipment tested/modified for use on the KC-135 and KC-10.

(4) **CSAR.** Tanker aircraft provide a limited capability to assist CSAR operations as a communications and coordination link between airborne and ground-based elements. This capability derives from the tanker's long endurance characteristics and organic communications equipment. In the case of a downed fighter, the wingman will attempt to remain on scene to ascertain the downed crewmen's status and provide protection until CSAR forces arrive. During this process, the tanker will normally remain at altitude, relaying information where communications connectivity is easiest, and will refuel on scene forces as required. During Operation ALLIED FORCE, KC-135s were diverted to the scene of a downed airman. Once on the scene tankers refueled two A-10 aircraft that were providing close air support for the rescue effort, AWACS aircraft providing C2 for the operation, and CSAR aircraft affecting the rescue.

4. **Planning Air Refueling Operations**

a. While many considerations for air mobility forces are the same for airlift and AR assets, there are some specific considerations unique to tanker operations. These include the following:

(1) **Boom Versus Drogue.** If planned operations will include a significant number of receivers requiring drogue-type refueling intermixed with receivers requiring boom-type refueling, planners should consider using tankers capable of both types of refueling on the same mission.

(2) **Total Offload Versus Booms in the Air.** Planners must consider whether planned operations will emphasize total offload capability for only a few receivers or a rapid refueling capability for multiple receivers. If total offload capability is more important (such as for large aircraft), fewer numbers of tankers with larger fuel loads should be planned. If the mission emphasis is on frequent, rapid refuelings to multiple receivers (such as multiple fighter strike packages), it is more effective to use a larger number of tankers maximizing the number of available "booms in the air."

b. **Daily Allocation.** At the operational level, force allocation consists of translating the JFC's air apportionment decisions into total number of AR sorties, by aircraft type, available for each operation or task. AR assets are matched against receivers in the ATO based on the JFC's air apportionment guidance but tempered by changing conditions. At this level, the most important decisions are those that place tanker aircraft types against receiver requirements, while optimizing the use of those assets.

c. AR capability can be increased without increasing the number or size of tanker aircraft by carefully matching tanker aircraft types against receiver mission requirements. This involves greater use of refuelable reliability tankers, assigning individual tankers to multiple receivers or receiver packages, and ensuring receiver AR requests accurately reflect their mission requirements. The considerations for daily allocation decisions are much the same as for contingency allocations as discussed above. When developing daily AR allocations, planners must consider boom versus drogue requirements, emphasis on total offload versus booms in the air, and SOF requirements.

d. **Airspace and ATC.** Many countries have specific restrictions on AR operations conducted within their sovereign airspace. Planners need to be aware of potential restrictions.

e. **Altitude Reservation (ALTRV).** Most intertheater AR operations require an ALTRV to reserve AR airspace. ALTRVs must be submitted IAW rules of the International Civil Aviation Organization (ICAO) in international airspace and must be submitted IAW ICAO and HN rules when conducted over territorial airspace. Planners must ensure ALTRV approval is received prior to conducting AR operations. ALTRVs do not relieve aircrews of the requirement to obtain diplomatic clearances or to file flight plans.

f. **AR Airspace.** Most intratheater AR is conducted in airspace specifically designated for AR. For peacetime operations, AR airspace is published in flight information publications with boundaries, altitudes, and communications frequencies agreed to by the ATC authorities. During a contingency, AR airspace close to the adversary will change frequently, and its altitudes and communications frequencies will be classified to avoid predictability. Routing to and from the AR airspace will also change in response to changes in air operations and adversary threats to friendly forces.

g. **Communications Capabilities and Emissions Control.** AR operations are highly dependent on both air-to-air and air-to-ground communications. Throughout AR operations, tankers must be able to communicate with their receivers, AWACS controllers, local ATC, and other tankers in formation and maintain at least a listening watch on designated high frequency channels. Mission requirements normally dictate that tankers maintain positive contact on most all of these frequencies simultaneously. Combat or politically sensitive missions may require both the tanker and receiver to exercise emission control (EMCON) procedures. These procedures minimize an aircraft's transmission of electronic signals (communication and navigation) to reduce the amount of information other forces can gather. Use of EMCON entails bringing two aircraft together, in the same airspace with an intentionally degraded communication and navigation capability. To be successful in refueling under EMCON conditions, standardized procedures must be developed between tanker and receiver(s). The procedures must be regularly exercised by both tanker and receiver aircrews, and they must be thoroughly briefed on the procedures to be used prior to each mission.

h. **Conditions.** AR forces and their receivers must be capable of conducting AR operations at night and under adverse weather conditions. Depending on the operation, this may require precision navigation equipment and night-vision capability.

CHAPTER VI
AIR MOBILITY SUPPORT

> *"Air power is not made up of airplanes alone. Air power is a composite of airplanes, air crews, maintenance crews, air bases, air supply, and sufficient replacements in both planes and crews to maintain a constant fighting strength..."*
>
> **General Henry "Hap" Arnold**
> **General of the Air Force (1949)**

1. General

The MAF's four core capabilities are airlift, AR, AE, and air mobility support/GAMSS. Successful employment of the airlift and AR force is contingent upon establishing and maintaining a GAMSS force that enables aerial deployment, employment, sustainment, and redeployment of US forces throughout the range of military operations. Specifically, air mobility support forces provide the responsive, worldwide foundation for airlift and AR operations. This force is divided between USTRANSCOM, which controls the majority of assets in its global/functional role, and the geographic CCMDs that control sufficient assets to meet their specific regional needs. These forces, combined with the interrelated processes that move information, cargo, and passengers, make up GAMSS. This structure consists of a number of CONUS and en route locations, as well as deployable forces capable of augmenting the fixed en route locations or establishing operating locations where none exist. These deployable forces are stationed both in CONUS and at select overseas bases, and are controlled by either AMC or one of the geographic CCMDs. Pre-positioning GAMSS forces at locations supporting sustained airlift or aerial refueling operations should be accomplished ahead of any combat force deployment.

a. The reduction in forward deployed forces following the end of the Cold War resulted in an increased dependence on air mobility to project US military presence throughout the world. In turn there grew an increased dependence on GAMSS to provide rapid global air mobility. The mobile forces of GAMSS enable the en route system to expand or contract as necessary, providing worldwide coverage and lending direct support to the rapid global air mobility concept.

b. GAMSS forces are drawn from active duty, USAF Reserve, and ANG components. Collectively, these components provide the forces that make up the fixed CONUS and overseas GAMSS organizations as well as the deployable forces stationed primarily in CONUS. These components support operations throughout the range of military operations.

2. Air Mobility Support

a. Various Service organizations support air mobility operations by providing the operational capabilities essential for APOD reception. The USAF, through AMC's air mobility squadrons (AMSs), aerial port flights, and CRFs, provide much of the operational and logistic support needed to receive arriving aircraft. Navy expeditionary air cargo companies unload aircraft and operate air cargo and passenger terminals. Through its cargo transfer capability, the Army provides the required support to interface with the CRF and begin the staging and onward movement phases for deploying personnel, equipment, and materiel. Specific Service organizations include:

(1) **Marine Corps Component.** During a major theater deployment, the Marine Corps force component commander or the Marine expeditionary force commander will activate a Marine air-ground task force deployment and distribution operations center (MDDOC) to coordinate all strategic, operational, and tactical lift requirements for land and air forces. Located within the MAGTF command element, the MDDOC assumes the responsibilities of the force movement control center. The MDDOC will conduct integrated planning, provide guidance and direction, and coordinate and monitor transportation and inventory resources as they relate to management of the MAGTF's distribution process. The MDDOC will coordinate all strategic lift to move the forces from the aerial and surface ports of embarkation to the aerial and surface PODs and will facilitate MDDOC representation at the theater JDDOC.

(2) **Army Theater Sustainment Command (TSC).** The TSC is the logistics C2 element assigned to the Army Service component command (ASCC) and is the single Army sustainment (less medical) headquarters within a theater of operations. It is responsible for executing logistics and distribution capabilities for port opening, theater opening, theater surface distribution, and sustainment functions in support of ARFOR. Additionally, the TSC may provide lead Service and executive agent support for designated common-user logistics to other USG departments or agencies, multinational forces, and NGOs as directed. The TSC manages theater distribution and executes distribution operations IAW ASCC component logistics staff officer priorities. It develops the ASCC's distribution plan and synchronizes material and movement management, and is also responsible for coordinating the protection of theater distribution nodes. The TSC can employ one or more expeditionary sustainment commands as an extension of its C2 capability; each expeditionary sustainment command provides rapidly deployable, regionally focused capability for executing logistic operations that are limited in scope and scale when compared to those the TSC can support.

(3) **Army Sustainment Brigades (SUST BDEs).** SUST BDEs are subordinate commands of the TSC. All SUST BDEs plan, synchronize, monitor, and control sustainment operations within their assigned area of operations. Depending on its assigned mission, a SUST BDE will primarily focus on theater opening, theater distribution, or sustainment functions. Theater opening functions set the conditions for effective support and lay the groundwork for subsequent expansion of the theater distribution system. The critical tasks for a SUST BDE in a theater opening role include: theater reception support, staging onward movement/distribution management; life support; and initial theater sustainment.

(4) Normally, an Army, Navy, or Marine Corps A/DACG assists the mobility forces in processing, loading, and off-loading deploying and arriving service component personnel and equipment, for the Army, elements of a MCT and an inland cargo transfer company typically operate the A/DACG. The capabilities of the A/DACGs are tailored based on the mission and military units performing aerial port operations. An A/DACG will:

(a) Coordinate and control the reception and/or loading of units for deployment and redeployment;

(b) Coordinate with the installation commander and the commander of each Service-deploying unit;

(c) Provide a liaison to the mobility force (normally the air terminal operations center; and

(d) Perform those functions when no mobility force is available.

b. In addition, HNS may be used to free up finite reception assets and minimize the logistic footprint at the APOD and/or APOE. Close coordination with HNS activities is necessary to balance the operational requirements of all organizations competing for limited resources.

CONTINGENCY RESPONSE SUPPORT: OPERATION ENDURING FREEDOM (1 JUNE–10 JULY 2010)

In February 2010, Airmen from the 571st Contingency Response Group (CRG) deployed to Mazar-e-Sharif (MeS), Afghanistan, tasked by Commander, United States Transportation Command (CDRUSTRANSCOM) to establish a forward logistics base in support of the 30,000-troop surge for Operation ENDURING FREEDOM. The 571 CRG was also tasked to provide command and control, aerial port, aircraft maintenance, security, air traffic control and logistical support (weather, intelligence, etc.). Working in conjunction with the 41st Transportation Company (TC) and Soldiers from the 82nd Sustainment Battalion (SB), the mission of this 250-member United States Transportation Command Joint Task Force-Port Opening (JTF-PO) team was to build a high speed logistics lane to facilitate the flow of US Army personnel, equipment and supplies into Northern Afghanistan and the onward movement to other provinces. To accomplish its mission, the JTF-PO would need to dramatically increase the throughput and movement velocity of the existing airfield at MeS, so that it could handle a significant increase in airflow, to include commercial and military aircraft. CRGs and rapid port opening elements (RPOEs) are intimately familiar with each other's capabilities because they train and exercise together during JTF-PO validation exercises like EAGLE FLAG. For this mission, however, the assigned RPOE was retasked to align with another CRG to support the humanitarian relief mission in Haiti after a devastating earthquake. With no other RPOE available, agreements were generated with the 82nd Airborne Sustainment Brigade that provided tactical control of the 41st TC and direct support of a team from the 82nd Support Brigade Headquarters Staff allowing the generating of an ad hoc JTF-PO. The 41 TC provided ground movement capability to transport cargo/personnel to a forward distribution node, while 82 SB provided passenger processing and in-transit visibility and an Army perspective during negotiations with Regional Command – North (RC-N) and host nation entities. The JTF-PO worked with their German International Security Assistance Force (ISAF) hosts, RC-N

---

leadership and Afghan military and civilian officials to ensure smooth airfield/ramp operations, security and communications. The JTF-PO also built a strong relationship with the Navy Seabee element that was invaluable in the structural building of the new cargo yard and fuel farms that were essential to mission success. Finally, the JTF-PO established a close working relationship with the joint special operations task force element that provided information and intelligence for JTF-PO operations and in return were provided a section of the cargo yard to be used as a forward area rearming and refueling point for their rotary wing assets.

For this mission, the JTF-PO remained under the operational control of CDRUSTRANSCOM, but worked in a direct supporting relationship with US Central Command (USCENTCOM). The JTF-PO worked closely with, and provided support to, multiple agencies including US Forces Afghanistan, RC-N of the ISAF, the USCENTCOM Joint Deployment and Distribution Operations Center, the Air Mobility Divisions at Air Forces Central Command and US Air Forces in Europe and 618th Air Operations Center (Tanker Airlift Control Center).

The JTF-PO at MeS ensured the expeditious movement of over 18,100 short tons and 8,700 passengers, handling 824 Air Mobility Command, Coalition and commercial aircraft across two ground operations areas while coordinating operations with multiple agencies. The JTF-PO delivered 530 mine resistant ambush protected all terrain vehicles to US counterterrorism, counterinsurgency forces at nine forward operating bases in Northern Afghanistan, providing vital life-saving equipment for the warfighter and ensuring the security of the northern distribution network.

Various Sources

3. Capabilities of Air Mobility Support

The capabilities provided by GAMSS are C2, aerial port, and aircraft maintenance. While the GAMSS functions at fixed locations are robust, the deployable assets are designed to be temporary in nature with a planned redeployment or replacement. En route locations are normally tasked to provide these services; however, basic and other support functions (combat support, life support, intelligence, etc.) can augment in-place operations, creating a more robust throughput and support capability. The level of support can be tailored to match the workload requirements. Consequently, deployable GAMSS forces can provide a method for expanding capabilities at an existing location or establishing capabilities where none exists. To ensure continuity of operations, appropriate planners should coordinate the replacement and redeployment of GAMSS forces early in the planning process and to allow GAMSS forces to reconstitute for follow-on operations.

a. **C2 of GAMSS Forces.** Air mobility support operations encompass both global/functional support as well as focused regional support. When GAMSS forces deploy to a GCC's AOR, command relationships should be specified, coordinated, and codified before operations begin. They should specify the type and degree of control exercised by commanders in the theater, the providing commander, and the associated C2 organizations.

(1) Whether OPCON is maintained by Commander, 18 AF (AFTRANS) or a GCC's COMAFFOR, GAMSS forces usually provide initial C2 to higher headquarters for deploying forces through organic, deployable C2 systems. In addition, they set up stand-alone C2 operations for airlift operations. GAMSS forces perform C2 functions on behalf of the higher headquarters at the local level to accurately plan, flow, and track air movements and provide ITV of equipment and passengers. C2 requirements may include various radio and SATCOM systems, as well as mobility mission planning and execution systems supporting their airfield operations as well as those of supported air mobility aircrews that may transit or operate from their location. AMC assigned mobility support forces normally use this capability to report to the 618 AOC (TACC), while theater assigned support forces normally report to their theater AOC.

(2) Timely exchange of information within, between, and among GAMSS components is critical to mobility operations. This includes the following:

(a) Geospatial intelligence for imagery, imagery intelligence, and geospatial information requirements.

(b) Airspace coordination and management requirements.

(c) Restrictions imposed at airfields.

(d) CRF, STT, AMLO, and ground force assault team requirements.

(e) Unique requirements such as security and command, control, and communications for nuclear weapons.

(f) Asset ITV.

(g) Cargo, hazardous materials, passengers, and patient information.

(h) Weather information.

(i) JIPOE products and exchange of current and early warning intelligence.

(3) One of the most important features of GAMSS is its support of ITV and mission following/planning. Commanders depend on accurate, timely ITV of assets to more efficiently manage those assets and associated supporting operations. Consequently, the effectiveness of GAMSS relies significantly on integration of ITV data into a comprehensive picture. Without such integration, the ability to achieve rapid global mobility is compromised. NOTE: In selected cases, SOF STTs can provide a limited initial C2 capability, both traffic control and aircraft reporting.

(4) Various computer and communications systems along with their associated databases and peripheral equipment are included as elements of GAMSS.

b. **Aerial Port.** An aerial port is an operating location, usually an established airfield, which has been designated for the sustained air movement of personnel and materiel.

Deployed aerial port operations are sized based on forecast workload requirements. GAMSS units possess a robust aerial port capability. GAMSS units are designed to establish and operate air mobility terminals and have the ability to onload and offload a set number of aircraft based on forecast workload requirements. In addition, GAMSS aerial port specialists provide expertise to establish marshalling yards and traffic routing for cargo, aircraft servicing, passenger manifesting, and air terminal operations center services. GAMSS aerial port personnel are also responsible for the transmission of departure and arrival information to IGC, to include movement manifests and ITV data provided electronically by the moving unit. Deployable GAMSS aerial port services are not designed for long-term sustained aerial port operations. Commanders and planners should plan to backfill these deployed units quickly to allow them to redeploy and reconstitute for further use.

   c. **Maintenance**

      (1) GAMSS aircraft maintenance support is based on resources of people, parts, and equipment leveraged from CONUS and OCONUS units. Planners and units receiving maintenance augmentation from GAMSS forces should consider supplementing maintenance capability as soon as practical to ensure sustained operations. Designed primarily to support mobility aircraft operations, deployable GAMSS maintenance units are not intended to provide sustained maintenance.

      (2) Deployable units providing aircraft maintenance capability are contingency support elements (CSEs) and maintenance recovery teams (MRTs). Maintenance CSE packages are tasked to established locations for a specified amount of time to provide limited support for specific mission(s) flow. CSEs are normally deployed as part of a CRF to set up or work from an austere location. Their capability is essentially limited to basic ground handling and routine servicing operations. MRTs are small teams consisting of specific maintenance specialties tasked to provide aircraft troubleshooting and repair for a specific aircraft requirement.

4. Global Air Mobility Support System Elements

   Several USAF MAJCOMs possess GAMSS elements. AMC GAMSS forces are aligned under the USAF Expeditionary Center's administrative control, with assets at fixed overseas locations, as well as CONUS-based deployable assets. Unless otherwise directed, Commander, 18 AF (AFTRANS) retains OPCON of deployed GAMSS forces.

   a. **GAMSS fixed assets** are sized, manned, and equipped to support peacetime common-user air mobility operation. Fixed assets consist of the following:

      (1) **Contingency Response Wing (CRW).** AMC has one CRW that is organized to produce deployable CRFs. The CRW as an organization does not deploy, however, it coordinates the readiness and deployment of subordinate contingency GAMSS elements providing expeditionary en route support, airbase opening, building partner capacity, rapid AMD augmentation and AMLO capability. These forces deploy on order from CDRUSTRANSCOM or 18 AF/CC. CRW elements are designed for a decreased transportation and logistic footprint to support short duration operations, or as a quickly

deployable force that can support mission requirements until a more robust unit can deploy for a longer duration. CRFs deployments do not normally exceed 45 days. Written approval from the commander with OPCON authority is required to use CRFs assets and personnel to support any non-primary mission requirement. The C2 of GAMSS elements follows the normal C2 pattern of air mobility forces. GAMSS forces either remain under their own CCDR's air component or, if they cross-theater boundaries, are presented either in support or are attached, at the discretion of SecDef.

(2) **Air Mobility Operations Wings (AMOWs).** AMOWs are located overseas and provide a single commander distinct mission capability with the appropriate level of authority to ensure response time and agility to meet changing theater requirements and support the CCDR.

(3) **Air Mobility Operations Groups (AMOGs).** AMOGs are located overseas and composed of AMSs. AMOGs formulate plans, establish procedures, and direct the administration of their subordinate AMS, operating locations, and detached units in support of operations. The AMOG provides logistics, intelligence, and air transportation planning to meet operational requirements.

(4) **AMSs.** AMSs are situated at key overseas en route locations to operate air terminal facilities in support of the DTS for numerous DOD common users. AMS personnel generate, launch, and recover air mobility missions and en route support aircraft. Each AMS operates an air mobility control center, which serves as the C2 conduit to the 618 AOC (TACC) for air mobility mission tracking.

(5) **Mobility Support Advisory Squadrons (MSASs).** MSASs assess, train, advise, assist, and equip partner nations to ensure they have the capacity to counter insurgencies, terrorism, proliferations, and other threats.

b. **GAMSS** deployable assets are tailored to meet mission requirements, designed for a decreased transportation and logistics footprint, and are not designed as long-term assets. Training for members of these deployable assets consists of CBRN and weapons training. These assets are equipped and manned to support the contingency and/or wartime air mobility operation. The deployable assets consist of the:

(1) **CRG.** The CRG is an organization tasked to deploy in order to secure, assess, open and initially operate airbases for the USAF component of their CCMD. The CRG may initially represent the senior USAF leadership and for this reason the CRG is normally commanded by an O-6. The groups consist of a standardized force module dedicated to the base opening task. This module includes a tailored section of all forces needed after seizure, or handoff from seizure forces, to assess and maintain security of an airfield, establish initial air mobility C2, and operate the flow of air mobility into and out of the airfield. CRGs may open the airfield for the USAF, another Service or even a MNF partner. To ensure continuity of operations, CRGs coordinate with USTRANSCOM, AFTRANS, theater COMAFFOR/JFACC staff, and follow-on forces to expedite and synchronize transfer of authority to sustainment forces and the development of host unit support agreements. CRGs are comprised of approximately 115 personnel with a capability to support a continuous

working MOG of two aircraft for 24-hour a day operations. CRGs may be augmented with various support forces to meet unique mission requirements such as Airborne Red Horse which provides initial airfield assessment and expedient construction/repair capabilities for some scenarios.

(2) **Air Mobility Operations Squadron (AMOS).** An AMOS trains and equips personnel to augment geographic AOC/AMD positions and provides personnel to manage assigned mobility forces in support of contingency operations, humanitarian efforts, and unilateral, joint, and combined exercises. AMOS personnel, when deployed to a geographic AOC/AMD will normally be under the direction of the AMD Chief and AOC commander.

(3) **CRE.** A CRE is an expeditionary C2 force responsible for providing continuous on-site air mobility operations management. It is a temporary organization commanded by a commissioned officer that deploys to provide air mobility mission support when C2, mission reporting, and/or other support functions at the destination do not meet operational requirements. In addition to providing C2 and communications capabilities, CREs provide aerial port, logistics, maintenance, force protection, weather, medical, and intelligence services, as necessary. CRE size is based on projected operations flow and local conditions. CREs are comprised of approximately 58 personnel with a capability to support a continuous working MOG of two aircraft for 24-hour a day operations.

(4) **CRT.** A CRT is an expeditionary C2 force that performs the same functions as a CRE, but on a smaller scale. CRTs are comprised of 11-30 personnel and normally led by

a non-commissioned officer. They provide a level of aerial port, maintenance, and C2 services capable of supporting a working MOG of one aircraft for 12-hour a day operations, with 24-hour C2 coverage.

(5) **CSE.** A CSE consist of personnel and equipment providing specific contingency support capability other than core C2 such as contingency air load planning team, joint air cargo inspection, or airfield survey team. They may be deployed as an element of CRE or CRT, or as a small scale, stand-alone capability. These teams may require base operating support (BOS).

(6) **USN Expeditionary Air Cargo Companies.** Navy's expeditionary air cargo companies are elements embedded in both active duty and reserve component Navy cargo handling battalions. They may augment the USAF's aerial port operators or conduct independent aerial port operations. They interface with Navy fleet logistics and AMC's air operations.

c. GAMSS capabilities include:

(1) C2;

(2) Aerial port;

(3) Aircraft maintenance; and

(4) Other CSEs.

(a) **Airfield Survey Team.** These personnel are trained and equipped to deploy to airfields, assess the capabilities of the airfield and its supporting facilities, and relay that information to the appropriate authorities who deploy any needed augmentation or engineer forces.

(b) **AMLO.** An officer specially trained to implement the TACS and to control airlift assets engaging in combat tactics such as airdrop. AMLOs are highly qualified, rated airlift officers with experience in combat tactics and assigned duties supporting US Army and Marine Corps units.

(c) **Airlift Control Flight (ALCF).** ALCFs are part of the GAMSS that are gained by AMC. Personnel deployed from the ALCFs perform the core C2 functions of a CRE or CRT. Additional capability beyond C2 such as aerial port and aircraft maintenance are sourced and tasked elsewhere (typically from the CRWs or various mobility wings).

(d) **En Route Patient Staging System (ERPSS).** ERPSS is a deployable asset for temporary staging, casualty care, and administration support during contingency operations. It is located at designated transportation hubs to support the en route care of patients in the AE system. EPaSS holding capability is 2-6 hours for patients in the tactical environment entering the patient movement system and up to 24 hours at en route strategic locations. The EPaSS requires logistical, clinical, ancillary medical, and administrative support from the supporting base. The EPaSS may be augmented with additional personnel and equipment to increase casualty staging capability as needed.

(e) **Security Forces.** Air mobility missions operate in areas where a threat may exist. To mitigate these threats and provide limited aircraft security when appropriate base defense forces are not present, AMC maintains deployable security forces called PR teams comprised of individuals trained and equipped to provide protection of the aircraft when transiting high-risk areas. These forces may be augmented by CCDR-controlled fly-away security teams, who are trained to meet requirements to detect, deter, and counter threats to personnel and aircraft at deployed locations by performing close-in aircraft security and advising aircrew on dealing with detainee personnel. These forces may be part of an airfield opening effort, but do not provide sustained primary airfield security.

OPERATION UNIFIED RESPONSE (14 JANUARY–20 FEBRUARY 2010)

On 12 January 2010, the country of Haiti was ravaged by a magnitude 7.0 earthquake that devastated the capital city of Port-au-Prince and caused an estimated 112,000 deaths and 194,000 casualties.

Special operations forces (SOF), including a special tactics team, from the Air Force Special Operations Command, Hurburt Field, Florida, arrived at Toussaint Louverture Airport on the evening of 13 January 2010 to conduct austere airfield operations. Within hours, United States Transportation

Command (USTRANSCOM) deployed a team to assess airfield status and prepare for the joint task force-port opening (JTF-PO) main body arrival. An Air Force assessment team was dispatched to Port-au-Prince. The 818th Contingency Response Group (CRG) assessment team consisted of a CRG commander, a lieutenant colonel to provide expeditionary mobility operations expertise, an airfield operations officer, two civil engineering pavement specialists, a communications specialist, and a security forces specialist.

Shortly behind this small team was the first real-world use of an entire Air Force CRG and Army Rapid Port Opening Element (RPOE) combined. The 817 CRG and 688 RPOE joined to form USTRANSCOM's JTF-PO. Their mission was to safely run aerial port operations and maximize humanitarian assistance throughput at the relatively small, single-runway airport. After waiting in the holding pattern of Toussaint Louverture International Airport in Port-au-Prince for 2.5 hours, the joint assessment team (JAT) stepped off the aircraft the morning of 14 January to chaotic conditions.

The parking area at Toussaint Louverture only had 10 spots for large aircraft. Prior to JAT arrival, aircraft were parked close together and the airfield was crowded with all manner of trucks and people resulting in dangerous aircraft ground operations. If an accident occurred on the airfield's only runway it could shut down the only major airport in Haiti - with disastrous consequences for the relief effort. The JAT immediately began inspecting the control tower, passenger terminal, and areas for the JTF-PO main body use immediately upon arrival. disastrous consequences for the relief effort. The JAT immediately began inspecting the control tower, passenger terminal, and areas for the JTF-PO main body use immediately upon arrival. disastrous consequences for the relief effort. The JAT immediately began inspecting the control tower, passenger terminal, and areas for the JTF-PO main body use immediately upon arrival.

A couple of hours after the JAT landed, the JTF-PO Commander and main body arrived on five C-17s. The team immediately began coordinating bed-down and operations efforts with the JAT, special operations forces (SOF), controllers special tactics teams, and Soldiers from the 688th RPOE. On the periphery of the busy airfield, the 26-man security forces (SF) team set up a layered defense of the damaged perimeter. It soon became apparent more SF assistance was needed. On 24 January, a squadron of SF airmen from the 820th Base Defense Group, Moody Air Force Base, Georgia arrived and began working alongside JTF-PO defenders to fully secure the airfield.

The JTF-PO brought order to the parking area by controlling the flow of aircraft. A CRG maintenance crew chief was assigned to the SOF special tactics teams who were directing aircraft ground and air traffic. This Airman's role was approving movement into the parking areas and assigning parking locations to arriving flights, preventing taxiway bottlenecks and delays. Within a day, this logistical solution doubled the number of aircraft transiting the airfield. Due to the myriad aircraft supporting the relief effort and a lack of compatible ground handling equipment, foreign aircraft were often unloaded by hand.

> **The JTF-PO airfield manager developed a close working relationship with his Haitian counterparts that proved invaluable to quickly and efficiently solving countless problems across the airfield. Based on this relationship and recommendation of Haitian airfield authorities, the prime minister of Haiti, Jean-Max Bellerive, transferred airfield management responsibility to the JTF-PO team.**
>
> **At its peak, the JTF-PO team unloaded and turned 170 cargo aircraft every 24 hours. During its 37-day mission, approximately 210 Airmen from the JTF-PO were responsible for processing 3,006 Aircraft, offloaded 15,450 short-tons of cargo, and evacuated more than 15,500 American citizens. Of the 3,006 aircraft, 44 percent were US commercial aircraft, 38 percent were international relief aircraft, and 18 percent were military aircraft.**
>
> **Joint Task Force-Port Opening (JTF-PO): Port-au-Prince, Haiti**
> **Various Sources**

5. Airfield Opening and Global Air Mobility Support System

a. GAMSS forces may be the first USAF presence on an expeditionary airfield regardless of how the airfield is gained (e.g., seizure or acceptance from a HN) or which follow-on US or multinational entity will operate the airfield. When opening an airfield, GAMSS forces normally coordinate actions with theater command elements to ensure theater-specific responsibilities, such as force protection, meet mission requirements. All deployed GAMSS forces should integrate with the host organization to the maximum extent possible for force protection and communications. Additional issues that should be considered during planning are: the handoff of the airfield from any seizure force to the CRG or other GAMSS element, the CRG/GAMSS element to follow-on sustainment unit or HN forces, and redeployment and reconstitution of the CRG/GAMSS.

b. **Air Mobility Support Planning**

(1) Successful deployment and employment of forces and materiel depend upon timely and accurate planning of all US and coalition supported and supporting components. GAMSS is an integral part of the air mobility force, and its integration into the initial deployment flow is critical to any effective contingency or crisis action planning processes. Although relatively small in numbers, GAMSS forces fill a vital niche, and successful accomplishment of air mobility operations hinges on this support. Defined areas of operations and responsibilities for GAMSS personnel should be specified during planning of seizure/airfield opening operations.

(2) These forward-deployed forces may augment the JDDOC in managing the deployment of intertheater and intratheater assets for the supported CCDRs and, when a contingency is complete, the redeployment of forces. Their effectiveness is directly related to a commander's understanding of a number of planning factors. Each factor needs careful consideration to ensure the GCC's requirements and objectives are achieved. All these factors are interrelated and, therefore, should not be considered in isolation. To ensure adequate support, coordination between GAMSS forces and theater planners should occur.

The following planning factors are not all-inclusive for every operation, but they give commanders the parameters involved in the proper use of GAMSS forces.

(3) **Fundamental Considerations.** Within the overall mobility support-planning framework, there are four fundamental considerations: task, threat, core capabilities, and timing.

(a) **Task.** Although specific circumstances and deployed locations may vary and the GAMSS composition will change, the operational task and purpose of the GAMSS remains constant. The basic requirement is to deploy GAMSS forces to a location where they either establish operations at a previously unsupported base or augment the in-place or permanent en route support system to conduct mobility support to worldwide common users. Worldwide taskings for GAMSS forces center on this operation. The fixed infrastructure is composed of CONUS and overseas en route locations. This entire network is the foundation for GAMSS operations and their locations provide C2, logistics, and aerial port services to meet DOD operational requirements. While air mobility aircraft are used to project power, GAMSS forces are the backbone of this power projection.

(b) **Threat.** CCDRs should always be alert to the possible threats facing GAMSS forces. This includes noncombat missions like humanitarian support missions. Forces may face threats to security from individuals and groups as well as military and paramilitary units. Threat assessments should be conducted in consultation with intelligence, security forces, counterintelligence forces, medical planners, interagency partners, and in-country diplomatic and defense liaison personnel. A provision for force protection is required for any operation. The threat assessment will determine the level of force protection required. It may be necessary to consider delaying deployments until the situation and area are stabilized. Threats can directly affect the flow of air mobility operations and objectives of the JFC. Although GAMSS forces are trained to protect themselves against both conventional weapons and CBRN threats and hazards, they should be augmented by a dedicated force protection element whenever the assessed threat affects operational success.

(c) **Core Capabilities.** The capabilities of the trained GAMSS forces are a fundamental consideration. These forces are finite resources with unique capabilities. They have multiple technical qualifications and are packaged as deployment modules. They train as modules, and every effort should be made to deploy them as such. This training, experience, and organization make them ready for autonomous operations in uncertain environments. Consequently, their finite nature drives the requirement for commanders to carefully manage their allocation against prioritized requirements. GAMSS provides C2, aerial port, and maintenance capability.

(d) **Timing.** The timing of force movements is a critical consideration. GAMSS forces usually preposition upon receipt of the CJCS warning/alert order. This early positioning enables effective airlift and aerial refueling operations. GAMSS forces are sequenced early in the TPFDD or deployment order (DEPORD) planning. For large-scale mobility operations, this early integration in the deployment flow ensures APODs are prepared to receive cargo and passengers.

c. **Planning Considerations.** There are additional planning considerations impacting throughput and affecting operation or campaign objectives.

(1) **Footprint.** The number of people, the amount of equipment deployed for an operation, and the physical space they occupy on the ground comprise the footprint of the force. The scale of any operation determines the footprint, but the proper balance of people and equipment and using the reachback concept can minimize the footprint of deployed forces. As footprint size increases, more airlift is required to support these forces and less airlift is available to meet other JFC requirements. Diplomatic restrictions may affect the size of a footprint. A HN may limit the number of foreign personnel on its soil, making the need for reachback support even more crucial. Paring and tailoring of forces based on the in-place infrastructure can also reduce the footprint. This reduction allows airlift assets to be reassigned for other priority taskings.

(2) **BOS also known as Expeditionary Combat Support (ECS).** GAMSS forces may deploy with limited or no organic BOS/ECS assets. Therefore the supported commander should be prepared to meet the additional requirements of GAMSS forces. If tasked to augment theater-assigned BOS/ECS personnel, the GAMSS force commander can plan for and deploy with additional support personnel.

(3) **HNS.** Deployed operations always rely to some extent on HNS. HNS can include diplomatic clearances, airspace access, lodging, food services, POL, water, communications, labor, or other types of support. Assessment of HNS capability and willingness is a critical consideration in the planning phases. Shortfalls in HNS are normally overcome through additional supply efforts including contract support. If this assessment is not accurate, forces will not have adequate support to conduct operations, or finite transportation capacity will be wasted on cargo already available at the deployed location. Use of HNS agreements can be an effective force enabler and force multiplier. Obtaining local labor support from the HN affords US forces economy of force. The force multiplying effect is the reduced airlift required for force support. Footprint size is also dramatically reduced when HN services and support are maximized. To comply with congressional oversight, HNS should be tracked and reported to the applicable command element.

(4) **Diplomatic Clearances.** Diplomatic clearances are crucial planning considerations. These types of clearances include aircraft overflight and landing rights, communications connection approval, personnel visas, and other entry requirements. No TPFDD, DEPORD flow, or sustainment channel mission can occur without appropriate clearances obtained in advance. Without these clearances, the ability of GAMSS forces to enable rapid global mobility can be halted. Diplomatic clearances impact footprint, throughput, force protection, and ultimately, operational success, and should be acquired prior to execution of a TPFDD or DEPORD.

Intentionally Blank

APPENDIX A
REFERENCES

The development of JP 3-17 is based upon the following primary references.

1. General

a. National Security Decision Directive Number 280, 24 June 1987, *National Airlift Policy.*

b. Executive Order 12148, 20 July 1979, *Federal Emergency Management,* as amended.

2. Department of Defense Publications

a. DOD Directive 4500.09E, *Transportation and Traffic Management.*

b. DOD Directive 4500.54E, *DOD Foreign Clearance Program (FCP).*

c. DOD Directive 5100.01, *Functions of the Department of Defense and Its Major Components.*

d. DOD Directive 5158.04, *United States Transportation Command (USTRANSCOM).*

e. DOD Instruction 4500.43, *Operational Support Airlift (OSA).*

f. DOD Instruction 5154.06, *Armed Service Medical Regulation.*

g. Defense Transportation Regulation (DTR) 4500.9-R, *Defense Transportation Regulation.*

h. DOD 4515.13-R, *Air Transportation Eligibility.*

i. *Unified Command Plan.*

3. Chairman of the Joint Chiefs of Staff Publications

a. CJCS Instruction 5120.02B, *Joint Doctrine Development System.*

b. CJCSM 3122.01A, *Joint Operation Planning and Execution System (JOPES) Volume I (Planning Policies and Procedures).*

c. CJCSM 3122.02 D, *Joint Operation Planning and Execution System (JOPES) Volume III (Time-Phased Force and Deployment Data Development and Deployment Execution).*

d. CJCSM 3130.03, *Adaptive Planning and Execution (APEX) Planning Formats and Guidance.*

e. CJCSM 5120.01, *Joint Doctrine Development Process.*

f. JP 1, *Doctrine for the Armed Forces of the United States.*

g. JP 1-02, *Department of Defense Dictionary of Military and Associated Terms.*

h. JP 2-0, *Joint Intelligence.*

i. JP 3-0, *Joint Operations.*

j. JP 3-02, *Amphibious Operations.*

k. JP 3-05, *Special Operations.*

l. JP 3-10, *Joint Security Operations in Theater.*

m. JP 3-11, *Operations in Chemical, Biological, Radiological, and Nuclear Environments.*

n. JP 3-13, *Information Operations.*

o. JP 3-16, *Multinational Operations.*

p. JP 3-18, *Joint Forcible Entry Operations.*

q. JP 3-30, *Command and Control for Joint Air Operations.*

r. JP 3-34, *Joint Engineer Operations.*

s. JP 3-35, *Deployment and Redeployment Operations.*

t. JP 3-41, *Chemical, Biological, Radiological, and Nuclear Consequence Management.*

u. JP 3-52, *Joint Airspace Control.*

v. JP 3-59, *Meteorological and Oceanographic Operations.*

w. JP 3-61, *Public Affairs.*

x. JP 3-63, *Detainee Operations.*

y. JP 4-0, *Joint Logistics.*

z. JP 4-01, *The Defense Transportation System.*

aa. JP 4-01.5, *Joint Terminal Operations.*

bb. JP 4-02, *Health Services.*

cc. JP 4-05, *Joint Mobilization Planning.*

dd. JP 4-09, *Distribution Operations.*

ee. JP 6-0, *Joint Communications System.*

4. Multi-Service Publication

FM 3-52.3/MCRP 3-25A/NTTP 3-56.3/AFTTP 3-2.23, *Multi-Service Tactics, Techniques, and Procedures for Joint Air Traffic Control.*

5. United States Army Publications

a. Army Doctrine Publication 3-0, *Unified Land Operations.*

b. Army Doctrine Reference Publication 3-0, *Unified Land Operations.*

6. United States Air Force Publications

a. AFDD 3-05, *Special Operations.*

b. AFDD 3-17, *Air Mobility Operations.*

c. AFDD 3-52, *Airspace Control*

d. AFDD 4-02, *Medical Operation.*

e. Air Force Instruction 13-1, *AOC series publications.*

f. Air Force Instruction 13-217, *Drop Zone and Landing Zone Operations.*

g. AFTTP 3-3 AOC, *Operational Employment-Air and Space Operations Center.*

h. AFTPP 3-42.5, *Aeromedical Evacuation.*

7. North Atlantic Treaty Organization Publication

ATP-56(B), *Air to Air Refueling.*

Intentionally Blank

APPENDIX B
ADMINISTRATIVE INSTRUCTIONS

1. User Comments

Users in the field are highly encouraged to submit comments on this publication to: Joint Staff J-7, Deputy Director, Joint Education and Doctrine, ATTN: Joint Doctrine Analysis Division, 116 Lake View Parkway, Suffolk, VA 23435-2697. These comments should address content (accuracy, usefulness, consistency, and organization), writing, and appearance.

2. Authorship

The lead agent for this publication is the US Transportation Command. The Joint Staff doctrine sponsor for this publication is the Joint Staff Logistics Directorate (J-4).

3. Supersession

This publication supersedes JP 3-17, 02 October 2009, *Air Mobility Operations.*

4. Change Recommendations

a. Recommendations for urgent changes to this publication should be submitted:

    TO: JOINT STAFF WASHINGTON DC//J7-JE&D//

b. Routine changes should be submitted electronically to the Deputy Director, Joint Education and Doctrine, ATTN: Joint Doctrine Analysis Division, 116 Lake View Parkway, Suffolk, VA 23435-2697, and info the lead agent and the Director for Joint Force Development, J-7/JE&D.

c. When a Joint Staff directorate submits a proposal to the CJCS that would change source document information reflected in this publication, that directorate will include a proposed change to this publication as an enclosure to its proposal. The Services and other organizations are requested to notify the Joint Staff J-7 when changes to source documents reflected in this publication are initiated.

5. Distribution of Publications

Local reproduction is authorized, and access to unclassified publications is unrestricted. However, access to and reproduction authorization for classified JPs must be IAW DOD Manual 5200.01, Volume 1, *DOD Information Security Program: Overview, Classification, and Declassification,* and DOD Manual 5200.01, Volume 3, *DOD Information Security Program: Protection of Classified Information.*

6. Distribution of Electronic Publications

a. Joint Staff J-7 will not print copies of JPs for distribution. Electronic versions are available on JDEIS at https://jdeis.js.mil (NIPRNET) and http://jdeis.js.smil.mil (SIPRNET), and on the JEL at http://www.dtic.mil/doctrine (NIPRNET).

b. Only approved JPs and joint test publications are releasable outside the combatant commands, Services, and Joint Staff. Release of any classified JP to foreign governments or foreign nationals must be requested through the local embassy (Defense Attaché Office) to DIA, Defense Foreign Liaison/IE-3, 200 MacDill Blvd., Joint Base Anacostia-Bolling, Washington, DC 20340-5100.

c. JEL CD-ROM. Upon request of a joint doctrine development community member, the Joint Staff J-7 will produce and deliver one CD-ROM with current JPs. This JEL CD-ROM will be updated not less than semi-annually and when received can be locally reproduced for use within the combatant commands, Services, and combat support agencies.

GLOSSARY
PART I—ABBREVIATIONS AND ACRONYMS

ACL	allowable cabin load
A/DACG	arrival/departure airfield control group
ADE	airdrop damage estimate
AE	aeromedical evacuation
AECT	aeromedical evacuation control team
AF	Air Force
AFDD	Air Force doctrine document
AFRC	Air Force Reserve Command
AFTRANS	Air Force Transportation Component
AFTTP	Air Force tactics, techniques, and procedures
AGL	above ground level
ALCF	airlift control flight
ALOC	air line of communications
ALTRV	altitude reservation
AMC	Air Mobility Command
AMD	air mobility division
AMLO	air mobility liaison officer
AMOG	air mobility operations group
AMOS	air mobility operations squadron
AMOW	air mobility operations wing
AMS	air mobility squadron
AMX	air mobility express
ANG	Air National Guard
AOC	air operations center
AOR	area of responsibility
APEX	Adaptive Planning and Execution
APOD	aerial port of debarkation
APOE	aerial port of embarkation
AR	air refueling
ARFOR	Army forces
ASCC	Army Service component command
ATC	air traffic control
ATO	air tasking order
ATP	allied tactical publication
AV	asset visibility
AWACS	Airborne Warning and Control System
BCD	battlefield coordination detachment
BDOC	base defense operations center
BOS	base operating support
C2	command and control
CAMPS	Consolidated Air Mobility Planning System

CBRN	chemical, biological, radiological, and nuclear
CC	component commander
CCDR	combatant commander
CCMD	combatant command
CDRUSTRANSCOM	Commander, United States Transportation Command
CDS	container delivery system
CE	circular error
CJCS	Chairman of the Joint Chiefs of Staff
CJCSM	Chairman of the Joint Chiefs of Staff manual
CJTF	commander, joint task force
COA	course of action
COCOM	combatant command (command authority)
COMAFFOR	commander, Air Force forces
CONOPS	concept of operations
CONUS	continental United States
CRAF	Civil Reserve Air Fleet
CRC	control and reporting center
CRE	contingency response element
CRF	contingency response force
CRG	contingency response group
CRT	contingency response team
CRW	contingency response wing
CSAR	combat search and rescue
CSE	contingency support element
DACG	departure airfield control group
DDOC	Deployment and Distribution Operations Center (USTRANSCOM)
DEPORD	deployment order
DIRMOBFOR	director of mobility forces
DOD	Department of Defense
DOS	Department of State
DTS	Defense Transportation System
DZ	drop zone
DZC	drop zone controller
DZST	drop zone support team
ECS	expeditionary combat support
EMCON	emission control
EOC	emergency operations center
ERPSS	En Route Patient Staging System
EW	electronic warfare
EZ	exchange zone
FM	field manual (Army)
FOB	forward operating base

GAMSS	Global Air Mobility Support System
GATES	Global Air Transportation Execution System
GCC	geographic combatant commander
GDSS	Global Decision Support System
GLO	ground liaison officer
GPS	Global Positioning System
HN	host nation
HNS	host-nation support
HVCDS	high-velocity container delivery system
IAW	in accordance with
ICAO	International Civil Aviation Organization
ICDS	improved container delivery system
IGC	Integrated Data Environment/Global Transportation Network Convergence
IO	information operations
ITV	in-transit visibility
J-4	logistics directorate of a joint staff
JA/ATT	joint airborne and air transportability training
JAOC	joint air operations center
JCS	Joint Chiefs of Staff
JDDE	joint deployment and distribution enterprise
JDDOC	joint deployment and distribution operations center
JENM	joint enterprise network manager
JFACC	joint force air component commander
JFC	joint force commander
JFSOCC	joint force special operations component commander
JIPOE	joint intelligence preparation of the operational environment
JMC	joint movement center
JOA	joint operations area
JOPES	Joint Operation Planning and Execution System
JP	joint publication
JPADS	joint precision airdrop system
JPEC	joint planning and execution community
JRSOI	joint reception, staging, onward movement, and integration
JTF	joint task force
JTF-PO	joint task force-port opening
LCADS	low-cost aerial delivery system
LNO	liaison officer
LRST	long-range surveillance team
LZ	landing zone

MAF	mobility air forces
MAGTF	Marine air-ground task force
MAJCOM	major command (USAF)
MC	mission-critical
MCRP	Marine Corps reference publication
MCT	movement control team
MDDOC	Marine air-ground task force deployment and distribution operations center
MHE	materials handling equipment
MILDEC	military deception
MOG	maximum (aircraft) on ground
MOPP	mission-oriented protective posture
MRT	maintenance recovery team
MTF	medical treatment facility
NAMS	National Air Mobility System
NEO	noncombatant evacuation operation
NIPRNET	Nonsecure Internet Protocol Router Network
NTTP	Navy tactics, techniques, and procedures
OA	operational area
O&M	operation and maintenance
OCONUS	outside the continental United States
OEF	Operation ENDURING FREEDOM
OIF	Operation IRAQI FREEDOM
OPCON	operational control
OPLAN	operation plan
OPORD	operation order
OPSEC	operations security
OSA	operational support airlift
PA	public affairs
PI	point of impact
PMR	patient movement requirement
PMRC	patient movement requirements center
POL	petroleum, oils, and lubricants
PR	Phoenix Raven
RAMCC	regional air movement control center
RV	rendezvous
618 AOC (TACC)	618 Air Operations Center (Tanker Airlift Control Center)
SAA	senior airfield authority
SAAM	special assignment airlift mission
SATCOM	satellite communications

SEAD	suppression of enemy air defenses
SecDef	Secretary of Defense
SIPRNET	SECRET Internet Protocol Router Network
SOF	special operations forces
SPM	single port manager
STO	special technical operations
STT	special tactics team
SUST BDE	sustainment brigade
TACON	tactical control
TACP	tactical air control party
TACS	theater air control system
TACT	tactical aviation control team
TDD	time-definite delivery
THX	theater express
TOC	tactical operations center
TPFDD	time-phased force and deployment data
TRIADS	Tri-Wall Aerial Distribution System
TS	time-sensitive
TSC	theater sustainment command (Army)
TTP	tactics, techniques, and procedures
TWCF	Transportation Working Capital Fund
USAF	United States Air Force
USC	United States Code
USEUCOM	United States European Command
USG	United States Government
USMC	United States Marine Corps
USN	United States Navy
USNORTHCOM	United States Northern Command
USTRANSCOM	United States Transportation Command
XCDS	Extracted Container Delivery System

aerial port. An airfield that has been designated for the sustained air movement of personnel and materiel as well as an authorized port for entrance into or departure from the country where located. Also called **APORT.** (JP 1-02. SOURCE: JP 3-17)

aeromedical evacuation control team. A core team assigned to a component-numbered air force air operations center air mobility division that provides operational planning, scheduling, and execution of theater aeromedical evacuation missions and positioning of aeromedical evacuation ground forces. Also called **AECT.** (Approved for incorporation into JP 1-02.)

airborne. 1. In relation to personnel, troops especially trained to effect, following transport by air, an assault debarkation, either by parachuting or touchdown. 2. In relation to equipment, pieces of equipment that have been especially designed for use by airborne troops during or after an assault debarkation as well as some aeronautical equipment used to accomplish a particular mission. 3. When applied to materiel, items that form an integral part of the aircraft. 4. The state of an aircraft, from the instant it becomes entirely sustained by air until it ceases to be so sustained. Also called **ABN.** (Approved for incorporation into JP 1-02.)

air delivery. None. (Approved for removal from JP 1-02.)

airdrop. The unloading of personnel or materiel from aircraft in flight. (JP 1-02. SOURCE: JP 3-17)

airfield. An area prepared for the accommodation (including any buildings, installations, and equipment), landing, and takeoff of aircraft. (JP 1-02. SOURCE: JP 3-17)

airhead. 1. A designated area in a hostile or potentially hostile operational area that, when seized and held, ensures the continuous air landing of troops and materiel and provides the maneuver space necessary for projected operations. Also called a lodgment area. (JP 3-18) 2. A designated location in an operational area used as a base for supply and evacuation by air. (JP 1-02. SOURCE: JP 3-17)

airland. Move by air and disembark, or unload, after the aircraft has landed or while an aircraft is hovering. (JP 1-02. SOURCE: JP 3-17)

air land operation. An operation involving movement by air with a designated destination for further ground deployment of units and personnel and/or further ground distribution of supplies. (JP 1-02. SOURCE: JP 3-17)

airlift capability. The total capacity expressed in terms of number of passengers and/or weight/cubic displacement of cargo that can be carried at any one time to a given destination by available airlift. (JP 1-02. SOURCE: JP 3-17)

airlift control team. A core team within the joint air operations center with intratheater airlift functional expertise to plan, coordinate, manage, and execute intratheater airlift operations in support of the joint force air component commander. Also called **ALCT**. (Approved for incorporation into JP 1-02.)

airlift mission commander. A commander designated when airlift aircraft are participating in airlift operations specified in the implementing directive. (Approved for incorporation into JP 1-02.)

airlift requirement. The total number of passengers and/or weight/cubic displacement of cargo required to be carried by air for a specific task. (JP 1-02. SOURCE: JP 3-17)

air mobility. The rapid movement of personnel, materiel, and forces to and from or within a theater by air. (Approved for incorporation into JP 1-02.)

Air Mobility Command. The Air Force component command of the United States Transportation Command. Also called **AMC**. (Approved for incorporation into JP 1-02.)

air mobility control team. A core team within the joint air operations center that directs or redirects air mobility forces in response to requirements changes, higher priorities, or immediate execution requirements. Also called **AMCT**. (Approved for incorporation into JP 1-02.)

air mobility division. Located in the joint air operations center to plan, coordinate, task, and execute the air mobility mission consisting of the air mobility control team, airlift control team, air refueling control team, and aeromedical evacuation control team. Also called **AMD**. (Approved for incorporation into JP 1-02.)

air mobility liaison officer. A rated United States Air Force mobility air forces officer selected, trained, and equipped to assess, train, advise, and assist with mobility air forces and ground force integration for air movement and sustainment. Also called **AMLO**. (Approved for incorporation into JP 1-02.)

air movement. Air transport of units, personnel, supplies, and equipment including airdrops and air landings. (JP 1-02. SOURCE: JP 3-17)

airport. None. (Approved for removal from JP 1-02.)

air refueling. The refueling of an aircraft in flight by another aircraft. Also called **AR**. (JP 1-02. SOURCE: JP 3-17)

air refueling control point. None. (Approved for removal from JP 1-02.)

air refueling control team. A core team within the joint air operations center that coordinates aerial refueling to support combat air operations or to support a strategic airbridge. Also called **ARCT**. (Approved for incorporation into JP 1-02.)

air refueling control time. None. (Approved for removal from JP 1-02.)

air refueling initiation point. None. (Approved for removal from JP 1-02.)

air terminal. A facility on an airfield that functions as an air transportation hub and accommodates the loading and unloading of airlift aircraft and the intransit processing of traffic. (Approved for incorporation into JP 1-02.)

allowable cabin load. The maximum payload that can be carried on an individual sortie. Also called **ACL.** (JP 1-02. SOURCE: JP 3-17)

chalk number. The number given to a complete load and to the transporting carrier. (JP 1-02. SOURCE: JP 3-17)

channel airlift. Airlift provided for movement of sustainment cargo, scheduled either regularly or depending upon volume of workload, between designated ports of embarkation and ports of debarkation over validated contingency or distribution routes. (Approved for incorporation into JP 1-02.)

Civil Reserve Air Fleet. A program in which the Department of Defense contracts for the services of specific aircraft, owned by a United States entity or citizen, during national emergencies and defense-oriented situations when expanded civil augmentation of military airlift activity is required. Also called **CRAF.** (Approved for incorporation in JP 1-02.)

combat control team. A task-organized team of special operations forces who are certified air traffic controllers that are trained and equipped to deploy into hostile environments to establish and control assault zones and airfields. Also called **CCT.** (Approved for incorporation into JP 1-02.)

common-user airlift service. The airlift service provided on a common basis for all Department of Defense agencies and, as authorized, for other agencies of the United States Government. (Approved for incorporation into JP 1-02.)

cross-loading. The distribution of leaders, key weapons, personnel, and key equipment among the aircraft, vessels, or vehicles of a formation to aid rapid assembly of units at the drop zone or landing zone or preclude the total loss of command and control or unit effectiveness if an aircraft, vessel, or vehicle is lost. (Approved for replacement of "cross-loading (personnel)" and its definition in JP 1-02.)

departure airfield. An airfield on which troops and/or materiel are enplaned for flight. (JP 1-02. SOURCE: JP 3-17)

departure point. A navigational check point used by aircraft as a marker for setting course. (Approved for incorporation into JP 1-02.)

director of mobility forces. The designated agent for all air mobility issues in the area of responsibility or joint operations area, exercising coordinating authority between the air operations center (or appropriate theater command and control node), the 618 Air Operations Center (Tanker Airlift Control Center), and the joint deployment and distribution operation center or joint movement center, in order to expedite the resolution of air mobility issues. Also called **DIRMOBFOR.** (Approved for incorporation into JP 1-02.)

dispersion. 1. The spreading or separating of troops, materiel, establishments, or activities, which are usually concentrated in limited areas to reduce vulnerability. (JP 5-0) 2. In chemical and biological operations, the dissemination of agents in liquid or aerosol form. (JP 3-41) 3. In airdrop operations, the scatter of personnel and/or cargo on the drop zone. (JP 3-17) 4. In naval control of shipping, the reberthing of a ship in the periphery of the port area or in the vicinity of the port for its own protection in order to minimize the risk of damage from attack. (JP 4-01.2) (Approved for incorporation into JP 1-02.)

drop altitude. The altitude above mean sea level at which airdrop is executed. (JP 1-02. SOURCE: JP 3-17)

drop height. None. (Approved for removal from JP 1-02.)

drop zone. A specific area upon which airborne troops, equipment, or supplies are airdropped. Also called **DZ.** (JP 1-02. SOURCE: JP 3-17)

dual-role tanker. An aircraft that carry support personnel, supplies, and equipment for the deploying force while escorting and/or refueling combat aircraft to the area of responsibility. (Approved for incorporation into JP 1-02.)

free drop. The dropping of equipment or supplies from an aircraft without the use of parachutes. (JP 1-02. SOURCE: JP 3-17)

free fall. A parachute maneuver in which the parachute is manually activated at the discretion of the jumper or automatically at a preset altitude. (JP 1-02. SOURCE: JP 3-17)

Global Air Transportation Execution System. The Air Mobility Command's aerial port operations and management information system designed to support automated cargo and passenger processing, the reporting of in-transit visibility data to the Global Transportation Network, and billing to Air Mobility Command's financial management directorate. Also called **GATES.** (JP 1-02. SOURCE: JP 3-17)

Global Decision Support System. The command and control system employed by mobility air forces that provides schedules, arrival and/or departure information, and status data to support in-transit visibility of mobility airlift and air refueling aircraft and aircrews. Also called **GDSS.** (Approved for incorporation into JP 1-02.)

heavy drop. None. (Approved for removal from JP 1-02.)

high-altitude low-opening parachute technique. None. (Approved for removal from JP 1-02.)

high velocity drop. A drop procedure in which the drop velocity is greater than 30 feet per second and lower than free drop velocity. (Approved for incorporation into JP 1-02.)

intertheater. None. (Approved for removal from JP 1-02.)

intertheater airlift. The common-user airlift linking theaters to the continental United States and to other theaters as well as the airlift within the continental United States. (Approved for incorporation into JP 1-02.)

intratheater. None. (Approved for removal from JP 1-02)

intratheater airlift. Airlift conducted within a theater with assets assigned to a geographic combatant commander or attached to a subordinate joint force commander. (Approved for incorporation into JP 1-02.)

jumpmaster. The assigned airborne qualified individual who controls paratroops from the time they enter the aircraft until they exit. (JP 1-02. SOURCE: JP 3-17)

landing zone. Any specified zone used for the landing of aircraft. Also called **LZ.** (JP 1-02. SOURCE: JP 3-17)

loadmaster. None. (Approved for removal from JP 1-02.)

low velocity drop. A drop procedure in which the drop velocity does not exceed 30 feet per second. (JP 1-02. SOURCE: JP 3-17)

marshalling. 1. The process by which units participating in an amphibious or airborne operation group together or assemble when feasible or move to temporary camps in the vicinity of embarkation points, complete preparations for combat, or prepare for loading. 2. The process of assembling, holding, and organizing supplies and/or equipment, especially vehicles of transportation, for onward movement. (JP 1-02. SOURCE: JP 3-17)

mobility. A quality or capability of military forces which permits them to move from place to place while retaining the ability to fulfill their primary mission. (JP 1-02. SOURCE: JP 3-17)

mobility air forces. Air components and Service components that are assigned and/or routinely exercise command authority over mobility operations. Also called **MAF.** (Approved for incorporation into JP 1-02.)

multipoint refueling system. KC-135 aircraft equipped with external wing-mounted pods to conduct drogue air refueling, while still maintaining boom air refueling capability on the same mission. Also called **MPRS.** (Approved for replacement of "multi-point refueling system" and its definition in JP 1-02.)

National Air Mobility System. None. (Approved for removal from JP 1-02.)

Navy-unique fleet essential aircraft. Combatant commander-controlled airlift assets deemed essential for providing air transportation in support of naval operations' transportation requirements. Also called **NUFEA.** (Approved for incorporation into JP 1-02.)

node. 1. A location in a mobility system where a movement requirement is originated, processed for onward movement, or terminated. (JP 3-17) 2. In communications and computer systems, the physical location that provides terminating, switching, and gateway access services to support information exchange. (JP 6-0) 3. An element of a system that represents a person, place, or physical thing. (JP 1-02. SOURCE: JP 3-0)

operational support airlift. Airlift movements of high-priority passengers and cargo with time, place, or mission-sensitive requirements. Also called **OSA.** (Approved for incorporation into JP 1-02.)

oversized cargo. 1. Large items of specific equipment such as a barge, side loadable warping tug, causeway section, powered, or causeway section, nonpowered that require transport by sea. 2. Air cargo exceeding the usable dimension of a 463L pallet loaded to the design height of 96 inches, but equal to or less than 1,000 inches in length, 117 inches in width, and 105 inches in height. (Approved for incorporation into JP 1-02.)

rapid global mobility. The timely movement, positioning, and sustainment of military forces and capabilities across the range of military operations. (JP 1-02. SOURCE: JP 3-17)

senior airfield authority. An individual designated by the joint force commander to be responsible for the control, operation, and maintenance of an airfield to include the runways, associated taxiways, parking ramps, land, and facilities whose proximity directly affects airfield operations. Also called **SAA.** (JP 1-02. SOURCE: JP 3-17)

618th Tanker Airlift Control Center. None. (Approved for removal from JP 1-02.)

staged crews. None. (Approved for removal from JP 1-02.)

station time. In air transport operations, the time at which crews, passengers, and cargo are to be on board and ready for the flight. (JP 1-02. SOURCE: JP 3-17)

stick commander (air transport). None. (Approved for removal from JP 1-02.)

strategic air transport. None. (Approved for removal from JP 1-02.)

supply by air. None. (Approved for removal from JP 1-02.)

unit aircraft. Those aircraft provided an aircraft unit for the performance of a flying mission. (Approved for incorporation into JP 1-02 with JP 3-17 as the source JP.)

withdrawal operation. A planned retrograde operation in which a force in contact disengages from an enemy force and moves in a direction away from the enemy. (Approved for incorporation into JP 1-02 with JP 3-17 as the source JP.)

JOINT DOCTRINE PUBLICATIONS HIERARCHY

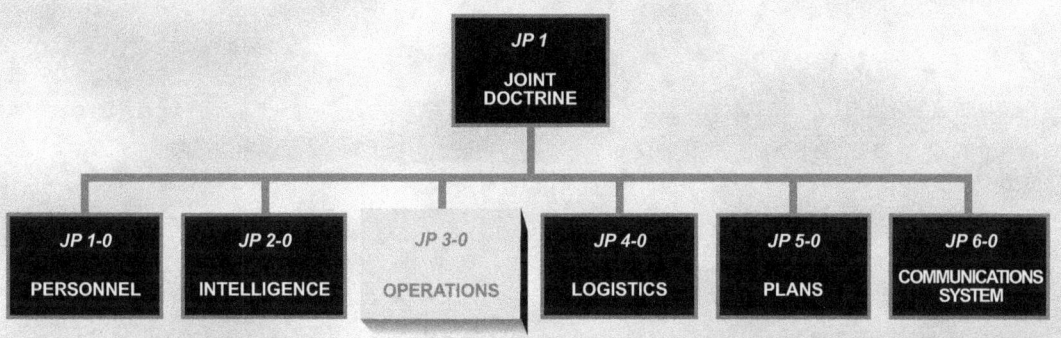

```
                    ┌─────────────┐
                    │    JP 1     │
                    │   JOINT     │
                    │  DOCTRINE   │
                    └─────────────┘
```

JP 1-0	JP 2-0	JP 3-0	JP 4-0	JP 5-0	JP 6-0
PERSONNEL	INTELLIGENCE	OPERATIONS	LOGISTICS	PLANS	COMMUNICATIONS SYSTEM

All joint publications are organized into a comprehensive hierarchy as shown in the chart above. **Joint Publication (JP) 3-17** is in the **Operations** series of joint doctrine publications. The diagram below illustrates an overview of the development process:

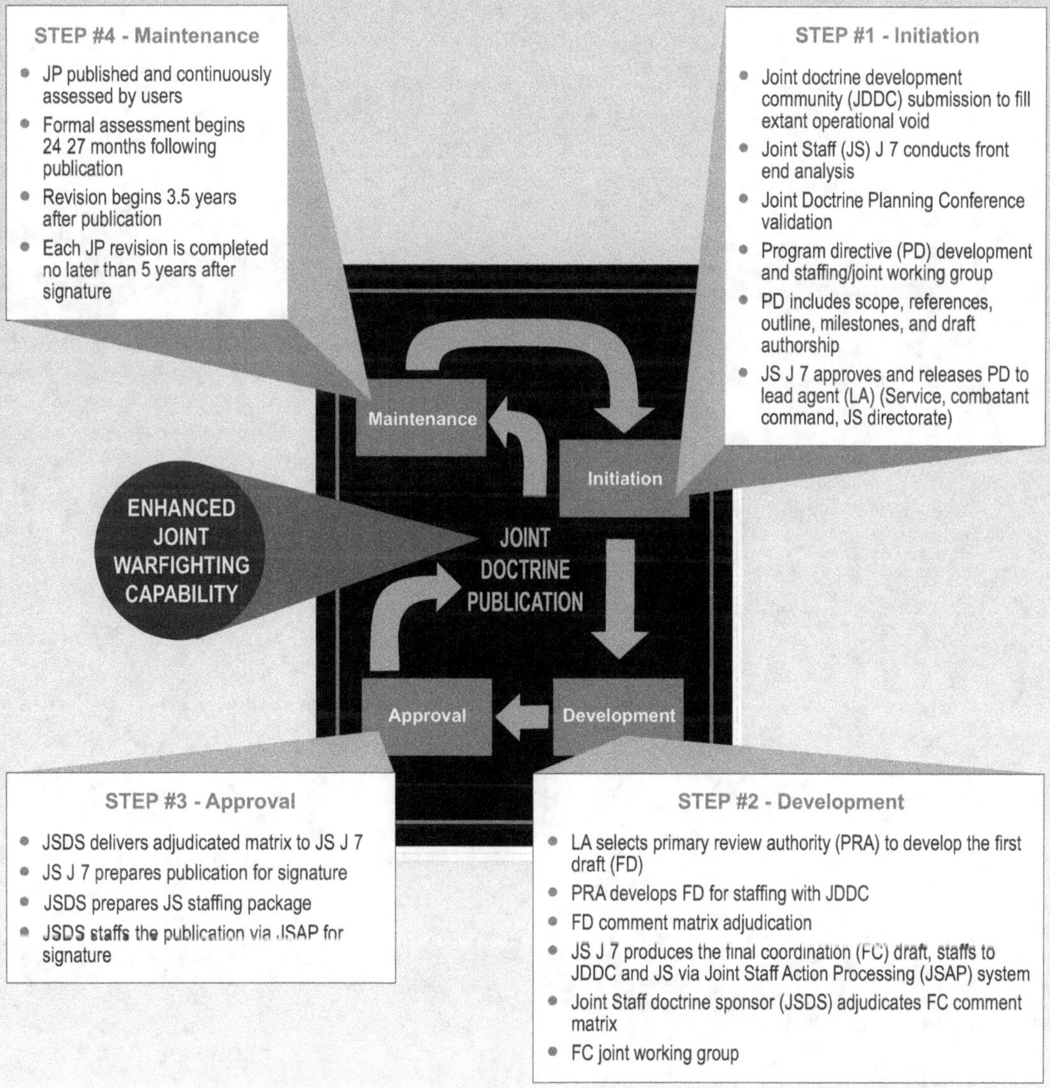

STEP #4 - Maintenance

- JP published and continuously assessed by users
- Formal assessment begins 24 27 months following publication
- Revision begins 3.5 years after publication
- Each JP revision is completed no later than 5 years after signature

STEP #1 - Initiation

- Joint doctrine development community (JDDC) submission to fill extant operational void
- Joint Staff (JS) J 7 conducts front end analysis
- Joint Doctrine Planning Conference validation
- Program directive (PD) development and staffing/joint working group
- PD includes scope, references, outline, milestones, and draft authorship
- JS J 7 approves and releases PD to lead agent (LA) (Service, combatant command, JS directorate)

ENHANCED JOINT WARFIGHTING CAPABILITY

Maintenance · Initiation · JOINT DOCTRINE PUBLICATION · Approval · Development

STEP #3 - Approval

- JSDS delivers adjudicated matrix to JS J 7
- JS J 7 prepares publication for signature
- JSDS prepares JS staffing package
- JSDS staffs the publication via JSAP for signature

STEP #2 - Development

- LA selects primary review authority (PRA) to develop the first draft (FD)
- PRA develops FD for staffing with JDDC
- FD comment matrix adjudication
- JS J 7 produces the final coordination (FC) draft, staffs to JDDC and JS via Joint Staff Action Processing (JSAP) system
- Joint Staff doctrine sponsor (JSDS) adjudicates FC comment matrix
- FC joint working group

www.ingramcontent.com/pod-product-compliance
Lightning Source LLC
Chambersburg PA
CBHW081325310526
45789CB00018B/2403